40
VERSES
to Ignite Your Faith

40

VERSES

to Ignite Your Faith

Surprising Insights from Unexpected Passages

Laurie Polich Short

BETHANYHOUSE

a division of Baker Publishing Group
Minneapolis, Minnesota

Published by Bethany House Publishers
11400 Hampshire Avenue South
Bloomington, Minnesota 55438
www.bethanyhouse.com

Bethany House Publishers is a division of
Baker Publishing Group, Grand Rapids, Michigan

Printed in the United States of America

Library of Congress Cataloging-in-Publication Data
Names: Polich Short, Laurie, author.
Title: 40 verses to ignite your faith : surprising insights from unexpected passages /
    Laurie Polich Short.
Other titles: Forty verses to ignite your faith
Description: Minneapolis : Bethany House, a division of Baker Publishing Group,
    2019.
Identifiers: LCCN 2018038660| ISBN 9780764232565 (trade paper : alk. paper) |
    ISBN 9781493417414 (e-book)
Subjects: LCSH: Bible—Criticism, interpretation, etc.
Classification: LCC BS511.3 .P645 2019 | DDC 248.4—dc23
LC record available at https://lccn.loc.gov/2018038660

Cover design by Rob Williams, InsideOutCreativeArts

Author represented by WordServe Literary Agency

In keeping with biblical principles of creation stewardship, Baker Publishing Group advocates the responsible use of our natural resources. As a member of the Green Press Initiative, our company uses recycled paper when possible. The text paper of this book is composed in part of post-consumer waste.

20 21 22 23 24 25   7 6 5 4 3

For all who seek God
and wisdom and hope . . .
and wonder where to go.

Contents

Contents

Introduction

God can sometimes be missing from where we would like God to be.

This observation keeps many people at a distance and can chip away at a believer's faith. After I wrote a book about my own experience of sitting in the silence of God, my inbox was filled with emails from people who needed encouragement in their waning faith:

Jessica asked why she should hold on to God when it felt like God had let go of her. She spent ten years serving in ministry, had her deepest prayer answered then stripped away, and she wondered why God had abandoned her. All she heard was silence.

Lauren asked if she should continue pursuing her dream career, when she experienced rejection at every turn. She believed God was directing her, held fast to the encouragement of Bible verses, and solicited prayers from people who affirmed her call. So far, all she had been met with was a string of closed doors.

David felt paralyzed by the Scriptures he had memorized (and taught to others) that seemed to have failed him. As he watched friends receive the healing he himself longed for, he was envious and disturbed. He wondered why God seemed to overlook him while granting others the desires of their hearts.

From these conversations, the same questions kept surfacing:

1. Why do the verses I read in the Bible fail to come true in my life?
2. How can I have confidence that God is near when my experience is that God is far away?
3. Are there any Scriptures that can speak to my experience of being fearful and disappointed, and encourage me to hold on to faith?

That last question was the impetus behind this book. For years, when I've spoken at conferences, people have said to me, "You highlighted a verse in the Bible I've never seen before." Enough of these comments showed me there was a need for someone to write about the lesser-known Scriptures that often go unnoticed. Be careful when you think, *Someone should do something.* It may end up being you.

In this book, I have sought to expose new or glossed-over verses that give us a better understanding of how God works. I have discovered that it is in the "in-between" verses—the ones that whisper rather than shout—that some mysteries about God become a little clearer.

My hope is that the insights in this book will provide you with new confidence when you experience the fear, disappointment, and silence that play an integral part of your relationship with God. The lesser-known Scriptures that we pass over help us discover new angles that can breathe life into our faith.

I believe there are times when God may be willing to temporarily risk your belief in order to deepen your understanding—for the purpose of ultimately strengthening the relationship you have. So if you have ever been in a place where you wondered if you could even believe anymore, you may be closer to God than you think. Read on and discover why.

1

The Subtle Insertion of Doubt

> ### GENESIS 3:3
>
> *But God did say, "You must not eat fruit from the tree that is in the middle of the garden, and you must not touch it, or you will die."*

I f you read this verse too fast, you'll miss it. But if you look closely, you will see the moment where doubt begins. The response from Eve to the serpent reveals how the strength of our faith is undermined or enforced by our perspective of the way God works. The serpent's motive seems clear from the start, evident in the way he phrases his question: "Did God really say, 'You must not eat from any tree in the garden'?" (Genesis 3:1). Looking back at Genesis 2:17, you can see the difference between the serpent's words and the boundaries God actually gave. There was one tree God asked Adam and Eve to refrain from; it was the first opportunity given to humanity to exercise free will. By introducing this choice, God gave Adam and Eve their first chance to obey.

This raises the obvious question: Why did God put the tree there to begin with? Because without it, Adam and Eve would be left with only previously selected alternatives, and offering a choice is the only way to introduce human freedom. In the garden, we see God setting the stage to woo rather than control humanity. Had God created a world without choice, Adam and Eve would be puppets for God to program rather than human beings for God to love. But the doubt-planting serpent takes God's gift of freedom and twists it, attempting to make the restriction bigger than it is: "Did God really say you must not eat from *any* tree?" The serpent knows what humanity has been discovering ever since: The bigger God's withholding feels, the more we are apt to succumb. *Why doesn't God make room for what I want to do?* we silently ponder, and if we dwell on these thoughts, our perspective of God morphs into a pleasure restrictor, dead set on keeping us from our longings. We become like teenagers who question parental boundaries and conclude that their parents are out to ruin their lives. Then they grow up and become adults and realize their parents were out to save their lives. "Becoming an adult" may be just what God is after in our souls.

> In the garden, we see God setting the stage to woo rather than control humanity.

Our longings can range from companionship to provision, success to pleasure, and the quick answers to all these things dangle in front of us, with only teeny compromises to overcome. We even become emboldened by focusing on God's "unreasonable" commands and use His denial of seemingly good things as motivation to plow ahead. Meditating on what happens next in these verses can help us turn the tide before it's too late.

"Did God really say you must not eat from any tree in the garden?" the serpent hisses, laying his picture of God as a tyrant out for display. Eve starts her response nobly, remembering immediately those were not God's words. But her memory of God's restriction adds words that show the wedge her doubt has begun to make: "God did say, 'You must not eat fruit from the tree that is in the middle of the garden, *and you must not touch it*, or you will die.'" With this small added phrase, Eve chooses to highlight and build upon what she cannot do. Rather than focusing on the life-giving reasoning behind the directive, the restrictive piece of God's command is emphasized and enlarged.

Oh, how we have been there. The co-worker who edges closer and treats you better than your spouse does. The drink offered at a well-deserved celebration in the midst of your recovery from addiction. That moment you want to shout out, "Why would God put this delicacy in front of me—and then expect me to refrain?" This is where the trouble begins and where the mindset of trust starts to decline.

What happens next is fast, and unless we take our time looking at Eve's process, we wonder how she decided to disobey so quickly. Her eyes are taken off God's benevolence and care and directed instead to the fruit of the forbidden tree, and that tree becomes her primary focus in the garden. It's like lingering at a bakery window trying to muster up the strength not to go in instead of making the best first choice of just looking away. The choices get harder as we go, making our focus the first real battleground.

Two verses later, Eve eats. Then she gives it to Adam (who, you can note, is with her), and he eats too. Such a small thing, eating from that tree. We may even feel that God shouldn't have made the tree's presence in the garden so tempting for them. How quickly we can move from accepting responsibility for our actions to blaming God for setting the stage for our choice, even though the consequences were shouting to us from the start. Sleep with that co-worker and your marriage will never be the same. Take that drink and your recovery will be set back. Lie to a loved one and your trust will always be questioned.

With the largeness of grace, there are always second chances, fresh starts, and new beginnings, but the consequences of not listening to God take up residence in our résumés. Those consequences move from their place in God's warning to being dealt with in our lives, and we now have to live with the unwanted "garments" our actions have brought us. Whether these garments are brokenness, addiction, heartbreak, or loss, we now have a new understanding of sin and separateness born by our experience.

Thankfully, the God of second chances takes our tattered résumés and invites us to become spokespeople for why God deserves our trust. And when we speak of what we now know by experience, it helps those who hear our testimonies choose wisely, and it reinforces the strength of our future faith. Especially when we can't see the immediate appeal in the right choice.

REFLECTION

1. What is the strongest temptation you've had to do something you knew you shouldn't do? Can you track the process of the temptation?

2. Is there a longing or desire you are living with right now that is causing you to doubt God's goodness?

3. How does Genesis 3:3 speak to the way you perceive God's boundaries? Does this reflection challenge you, or does it enforce what you already believe?

2

Moving ahead of God's Timing

GENESIS 16:2

[Sarah] said to Abram, "The Lord has kept me from having children. Go, sleep with my slave; perhaps I can build a family through her."

She has waited long enough. Living endless days with an unmet longing has caused her glimmer of hope to move her to urgency. She can no longer sit in the silence of her prayer. She heard the promise God gave her husband and likely celebrated that an heir would finally come. As months have turned into years, however, Sarah questions whether God's strategy for causing this birth to happen might include her assistance. Sarah is my girl. When the going gets tough, the tough take control—especially when the perfect solution is directly in your view.

Her thought process is not unlike our own. During a long season of waiting or suffering, we may see a vision for how things could change, so we rush in and grab it. We spiritualize our actions by thinking, *Surely, God needs my help*, and subtly manipulate our circumstances to achieve a desired end. Years spent waiting with an unmet longing can subdue our faith, and we subconsciously begin to believe that life only becomes what we make it. Our prayers move from "God, do what only you can do" to "God, bless me as I do it," and we slowly drift to a functional atheism. Perhaps Sarah has not gotten to that point. But the disappointment she feels toward God is clear in the language she uses: "The Lord has kept me from having children." There are so many ways she could have stated her condition, but the way she describes herself reveals what she believes. And maybe more importantly, what she *can't* believe because of it.

> Our prayers move from "God, do what only you can do" to "God, bless me as I do it," and we slowly drift to a functional atheism.

Trusting a God who has allowed disappointment and despair requires a big faith. Many of us are tempted to give up hope, yet God urges us on with opportunities to trust. The Bible reveals that we have a God who will pull out all the stops for us to experience the largeness of His presence, even after we've attempted to shrink Him out of our lives. It seems God longs—almost desperately—for us to see how big of a God we have and what He is able to do. God knows that when things happen when we want them to happen, we celebrate. But when things happen after we think it's too late for them to happen, we worship. Only when it's too late, too hard, or flat-out impossible does God have the opportunity to emerge from the mist and come spectacularly into view.

God had proclaimed to Abraham that this heir would come to him *from Abraham's body* (see Genesis 15:4). Sarah's body is not specifically mentioned in the promise, leaving room for the alternative that she suggests. Perhaps Sarah thought God meant that Abraham was *supposed* to have this child through their maidservant. Building a family through wives and maidservants was perfectly acceptable in that culture; we see examples of it throughout the Old Testament. So it is important to note that Sarah is not suggesting anything deviant or wrong in her solution. I imagine the fact that Hagar was a servant in their household when Abraham got his promise may have even spurred Sarah into thinking, *That is why she is here! God wants her to help.*

On they went with the plan, Abraham consenting without a fight. I have often pictured him when Sarah suggested it. "Really, sweetheart? Sleep with that beautiful younger woman?" I'm guessing there was at least some appeal for Abraham, made evident by his quick response: "[Abraham] agreed to what [Sarah] said." Both of them must have felt they could not wait any longer for God to fulfill His plan, so they decided to fulfill it for Him. God allowed their plan to move forward—suggesting that His sovereignty and our actions mysteriously coincide. This dance between God's sovereignty and human will is evident in the presence of all sorts of things that seem outside of God's will that are nonetheless present in our complex world. The stories in the Bible illustrate that God's overall plan is secure; but the way we get there includes our participation.

So what clues to the mystery of God's actions and our responses do we find hidden in these verses? First, God is revealed more in what He *doesn't* do and allows than in what He *does* do and doesn't allow. We see here that we have freedom to move ahead of God in His timing, which seems like an oxymoron, since God is everywhere at once. Nevertheless, we exist within the confines of time, and God often uses His timing to increase our faith. By giving Abraham this promise of an heir, and then waiting more than ten years to deliver it, God was giving Abraham—and especially Sarah—an unwelcome opportunity to stretch their trust. This verse reveals their inability to continue waiting as the number of their years raced ahead.

I have lived their desperation, and I imagine that you have lived it too. Somehow waiting is necessary to grow our faith, and our

19

increasing faith is what God desires most. This is an ongoing lesson, because even when we see God deliver the impossible after a long wait, we don't usually welcome that opportunity again. Rarely have I beseeched God to slow down (with the exception of when I'm looking in a mirror as I age), but the times I've beseeched God to speed up are too numerous to count. When time goes on and I hear silence, like Sarah, I fill God's silence with my own solutions. Often those solutions even carry spiritual undertones as I pray God's blessing on my process in moving ahead. This verse, read in context with what happens next, encourages me to go another route.

Abraham and Sarah's move eventually does incur God's voice, but it is directed to Hagar after their plan goes awry. But this dear couple eventually sees that grace prevails even in detours. With a second chance to produce a promised heir, even after the fallout of their actions, Abraham and Sarah discover that God's overall plan is not derailed when we go our own way. This is especially comforting to those of us who have taken detours ourselves and wonder if good can still come.

REFLECTION

1. Where have you most recently experienced waiting in God's silence?

2. Are you tempted by a solution that seems less than perfect but is something you may settle for because you can't wait any longer for God to show up?

3. How does this story speak to your own life and situation right now?

3

Never Alone

GENESIS 16:13

*She gave this name to the Lord who spoke to her:
"You are the God who sees me," for she said, "I
have now seen the One who sees me."*

Her fate seems to be sealed. The people she has served have used her. She has been a pawn in her employer's quest for control. There is no story that captures the heart of someone who has been used, abused, or unfairly treated more than the story of Hagar; but it is Hagar's declaration that gives us our hope: "You are the God who sees me."

Hagar speaks these words in the middle of the desert, in the middle of being cast out, in the middle of quieting the cries of her starved, pregnant belly. She was compelled by her mistress, Sarah, to become impregnated by Sarah's husband, and now unwillingly carries a baby she'll be forced to give up. When Sarah realized Hagar was not a happy participant in her ploy, she complained to

Abraham about Hagar's attitude. He told her to do with Hagar "whatever you think best" (v. 6). These dismissive words are all that are recorded from the man Hagar gave herself to, the one whose seed is growing inside her. And with Abraham's permission, Hagar was mistreated—possibly even beaten—until she ran away.

This is not a flattering scene in Abraham and Sarah's story, but it is an important one. It reveals that God follows the marginalized, even in the middle of a story about someone else. The fact that this chapter in Genesis follows Hagar into the desert, rather than staying with Abraham and Sarah in their pregnancy quest, shows us that God is concerned about those who have been used, abused, or discarded by others. This story speaks to the loyal employee who is suddenly fired, or the spouse who gives her best years to her husband, only to be replaced. Perhaps it even dares to reach out to those who have had their bodies and lives stolen in terrible and secret ways and who wonder if there is anyone "out there" who knows their plight. *You are the God who sees me.* *Even if no one else knows what I have been through, I can have hope you are there.* These words are the gift Hagar gives to our faith—faith in the God who follows her in her difficulty.

God pursues Hagar in that desert and begins a conversation with her through an angel so that she knows He is there. Then God gently allows her to pour out her heart about her injustice and foreseeable fate. Hagar can't see her way out of the despairing circumstances that surround her, and she doesn't know what God sees about the way her circumstances will unfold. Tenderly, the angel speaks words of promise to Hagar about her child's future, and although the prophecy about her son is not all good news, it points to a new chapter of life and hope. Hagar's story will not end in the desert, and her boy will be hers to raise. This is a future and a joy for which she never could have hoped.

"You are the God who sees me," Hagar cries out, and it becomes a cry for all of us when we feel lost and alone. Our story won't be merely what we see in this set of current circumstances; and there will be both joy and sorrow as our future unfolds. We live the good and bad of others' choices as well as our own, but we are never alone. Hagar would not leave the desert and have a perfect life. Suffering and joy are part of the human experience; but Hagar's words reveal that we do not face any of these things alone. God is our company in our sufferings. Hagar's encounter with the angel in the midst of her despair affirms that truth.

There is another angle to this story—what it reveals about God's sovereignty. Here in this complicated story of Hagar, Abraham, and Sarah, we discover that God writes His story with us—not apart from us—and He includes the messiness of our choices in the way His stories unfold. While God's ultimate will for a son to be born to Abraham and Sarah is not shaken, Hagar's son will be grafted into their unfolding story. Given the history of the Arabs and Israelis following these two births, it would be easy to conclude that God's story would have been cleaner and simpler if Hagar had died in that desert, or if Ishmael hadn't been born. But this account reveals the inclusion of human intervention in our stories of faith. God preserves our freedom and gives grace to the victim; and He includes our mistakes in the outcome rather than wiping them out.

> God writes His story with us—not apart from us—and He includes the messiness of our choices in the way His stories unfold.

One wonders what happens after the angel tells Hagar to go back, submit to Sarah, and have her baby. I imagine as the years pass, Sarah may soften toward Hagar, possibly when her own eventual pregnancy takes place. One thing we know is true: The fact that this sidebar is included in the grand Genesis story reveals the important fact that God doesn't sweep away our messes; He includes them for how they will instruct us and others in our walks of faith.

Abraham and Sarah are still used by God in spite of their mistakes; Hagar is not forgotten in her pregnancy; and this short encounter between Hagar and the angel in the desert is a sweet reminder of the way God pursues us when we feel lost. We are not alone or abandoned in our sufferings. *The God who sees us* will put us on a path to find our way home.

REFLECTION

1. Where do you need to know you are seen by God right now in your journey?

2. Have you ever felt used or abandoned by people you loved (or served) and wondered if God cared? How does Hagar's story encourage you?

3. Have you experienced a wrong turn in your life (that you or someone else made) that God included and "recalculated" in your spiritual journey? If so, when?

4

Remembering and Living Our Waits

> ## GENESIS 41:1
>
> *When two full years had passed, Pharaoh had a dream.*

When two full years had passed," Genesis 41 opens, and we immediately move on in the passage to what happens next. But taking a minute to live in that phrase helps us appreciate the actual time needed for our stories to unfold. The story of Joseph can encourage us in a different way when we pause over verses like this one, especially when we consider what it took to actually live the story out.

The problem we can have with many of the Bible's faith stories is that we hear them in a thirty-minute sermon or Bible study and feel the rush and excitement as we watch God move—but we forget to take in the immense weight that lives in these six small words: "When . . . two . . . full . . . years . . . had . . . passed." For two years Joseph lived, forgotten, in a jail cell. Two years of checking off monotonous days and nights that passed without end. And let's not forget the word *full* in case *two years* passes too quickly off your tongue.

Some things that need to happen in our lives can only be accomplished through time. When God wants to work in us, through us, or around us, these time lapses are integral for how our stories will unfold. Joseph's circumstances shaped his character to prepare him to be the leader he would one day become; and having to persevere in his trial was the only way these character qualities could be developed. Events also needed to unfold around Joseph to pave the way for the job he would be hired to do, and we only see how these things lined up when we look back. There is a secret we need to remember about time—the waits that seem endless now will one day be seen as necessary for what they brought us, and we will recognize their value in our spiritual growth.

> The waits that seem endless now will one day be seen as necessary for what they brought us.

Joseph's story actually begins when he is a cocky teenager, proclaiming his dreams of grandeur to his unenthusiastic brothers, and we observe in Genesis 37 that God has some work to do to humble this future leader. Joseph's trials start to unfold when his jealous brothers sell him into slavery, and we see the first glimpse of his maturing character when he resists the advances of his master's wife. But instead of being rewarded for his strength, he is falsely accused of rape and sent to jail. Joseph has already logged some time in captivity before being moved to a prison cell, and he continues to be unfairly treated at every turn. What we see looking back on Joseph's story, however, is that each seemingly bad turn was positioning him for the good that would ultimately come. In this, we find our hope.

Sometimes the way up is down, and one of the strengthening aspects of Joseph's story is that it shows all that he goes through before he lands. But we have to slow down and live the timing of his story to fully receive what it has to give. Just before the phrase "when two full years had passed," we have every indication that things are about to change—Joseph has settled into being an obedient prisoner and finds himself imprisoned with two of Pharaoh's attendants. We hold our breath, especially since we remember his dreams in chapter 37 and have a sense that these two fellow inmates will be key to his rising to power.

But this is where the timing of the story takes a turn. After accurately interpreting the two men's troubling dreams, Joseph asks the cupbearer to remember him when he gets out of jail; but in the last verse of chapter 40, we get the despairing news that Joseph doesn't know: "Pharaoh's chief cup-bearer, however, forgot all about Joseph, never giving him another thought" (NLT). Since Joseph doesn't know what we know, I imagine for the first year, his persevering hope sustains him. But the second year undoubtedly brings feelings of hopelessness and despair. Scripture is silent, but I believe it is likely that Joseph gives up on the cupbearer's remembering him *just before* the cupbearer's memory is restored. In this timing of events, we can glean insight for our faith. We can't always see what might be directly ahead, and when we are living our own seasons of endless darkness, this part of Joseph's story can infuse us with hope.

We cannot grow our faith if we aren't given a chance to exercise it, and these time lapses in Joseph's story give him that opportunity. Once God moves, it is quick, and we almost forget the long periods of waiting that precede these moments. Pharaoh's troubling dream stirs the cupbearer's memory, and within hours we find Joseph's prison sentence taking a dramatic turn. The prison cell turns out to be his road to the palace; had he not been there to meet the cupbearer, this connection would not have been made. Egypt's drought is integral to Joseph's rise to power as well, so the wait in jail has to happen to line up the circumstances for Joseph to be called. Seeing the big picture of the story helps us understand all that happened—even while much of it seemed unfair along the way.

Hovering over "When two full years had passed," we understand what it takes to live out our faith. Joseph's dream of leadership ultimately did come to pass, but only after it looked like it wouldn't, and it is in that confusion and darkness where faith is lived out. When I got engaged—and then unengaged—in my forties after a long season of singleness, I wondered how God could bring me so close to my dream and then take my hope. Years later, I saw the story differently. Joseph's story was pivotal in my journey of faith. Perhaps it will speak to your life too.

REFLECTION

1. Are you waiting for something right now? If so, do you feel discouraged or encouraged in your wait? How does this verse speak to you?

2. Have you ever looked back on your story and seen more of what God was up to in your circumstances? If so, when?

3. Where do you feel tempted to give up? How does Joseph's story encourage you to see your circumstances and timing in a different way? If you look more closely at what was happening in you or through you, what do you observe?

5

The Sign Comes
after You Obey

A sign is supposed to come before something happens. Technically, that's what makes it a sign. But this little verse tucked into Exodus 3 shows us that when it comes to our faith, God wants us to be able to step out and trust Him without a sign. The sign comes in the form of God's faithfulness when we look back.

Moses is an eighty-year-old shepherd when God meets him in a burning bush, and their dialogue begins with God proclaiming what He wants to do through him. After the initial shock, Moses learns he will merely be the vessel for what will happen; the rescue of the Israelites God asks Moses to lead will be orchestrated by God. In verse 8, God says that He has "come down to rescue" the Israelites, language that includes certainty. Moses learns that the success of this mission will not be buoyed by any sign for the future; instead, it will be entirely dependent upon his ability to trust.

> The sign comes in the form of God's faithfulness when we look back.

Moses's initial response to God's mission is framed around his own inabilities: "Who am I that I should do this?" (see Exodus 3:11). God doesn't answer Moses's question, because it is the wrong question. God's response, "I will be with you," is saying that in the promise of God's presence, Moses must find his confidence and strength. Moses isn't quite ready to pack his bags; he has more questions before he can be convinced. As he thinks about approaching the leader of Egypt, he continues to ask for future assurance. When God says, "I AM WHO I AM" (v. 14), He is communicating that Moses will get the assurance he needs when he is there. Just as God is with Moses there at the bush, God will be with Moses when he gets to Egypt. Moses will get what he needs the moment he needs it, because the God of the present will accompany him there.

I don't know about you, but when I face uncertainty or fear about what is ahead, like Moses, I try to get confidence from God for what I will need. But this passage gives us the insight that we are called to trust God to be with us in our journey of faith. What is ironic is that after God tells Moses he will not get his sign until after he moves out in faith, God does many miraculous signs to compel Pharaoh to release the Israelites. Yet with each supernatural act—whether it's a plague of frogs, gnats, locusts, or blood—we see that no miraculous sign can ultimately convince Pharaoh to believe. Even after he witnesses all these miracles, he still doesn't believe God will do what He says.

It is fair to conclude from this passage that signs don't bring us faith; they merely serve to underline what we already believe. The most compelling signs are revealed to us *after* faith is exercised, not before, because only in looking back do we see all that God did. Moses will have to act on faith first, and when he takes the Israelites out of Egypt, the sign he has asked for will be seen in the faithfulness of their success.

There is another significant word choice in this verse. God says to Moses, "This will be the sign to you. . . . : *When* you have brought the people out of Egypt"; God does not say, "*If* you have brought the people out of Egypt." God seems to have no doubt in Moses and invites Moses to gain his confidence through God's trust. Moses is given assurance that what God says Moses will do *will* happen. God indicates that Moses will do this *before* Moses has even decided—and this gives us great comfort as we think about God's faith in us. God believes in us before we believe in ourselves, and when He chooses us for a task, He is willing to stake His success on our response. All we have to do is believe God for what will happen.

Moses's success will depend on God's power, so God has only one requirement of Moses: absolute trust. That is all Moses will need to accomplish the mission God has in mind. If God had given Moses a sign in advance to boost his confidence, it might have taken away from the relational trust God needs Moses to have, because Moses might have trusted his sign instead of leaning on God. With only the promise of God's faithfulness, Moses is relegated to ongoing dependence throughout his task. This may be the most important insight of this passage when it comes to our faith. God wants to be with us to lead us, rather than merely to send us, and the stronger our relationship with God is, the more we can do. Faith missions only fail when they never take place.

It is worthy of reflecting on the promise of this verse and whether we've missed opportunities because we couldn't trust God to carry us through. Risk is part of the journey, and each time we step out *with* our fear, our faith grows. Our faith isn't strengthened by getting what we need in advance, but by watching God deliver it when we need it. And each time we watch God come through, it becomes one more sign to strengthen our belief.

REFLECTION

1. Have you ever asked God for a sign to give you courage to do something? How does this passage speak to you?

2. What signs of God's faithfulness do you see when you look back on your life? Do you keep track of what God has done so you can remember His faithfulness for the future? If not, how can you start doing that?

3. In what area of your life is God asking you to trust Him for what is ahead? Is there something He wants you to do or something that is happening? How can you use this as an opportunity to grow your relationship with Him?

6

Manna, Maggots, and Trust

> ## EXODUS 16:19
>
> *Then Moses said to them, "No one is to keep any of it until morning."*

M oses gives the Israelites only one guideline about the food God provides in the wilderness: Keep it for only a single day. Through this simple directive, the Israelites learn that the manna God gives them is for their present need, not a future need. They will have to trust God to provide tomorrow the same way He did today.

But some of them just can't do it.

Oh, how I feel their pain, and perhaps you do too. In times of uncertainty and risk, we are tempted to grab on to what we have—and make sure we have enough for what we perceive our future will need. It seems irresponsible *not* to save, we tell ourselves, and while it's true that we shouldn't be careless with our provision, we diminish the real reason we cling. In our hearts we often recognize that it is fear or worry that drives us, and this is what we are confronted with in this passage. God doesn't want us to be led by fear or worry, and He will continue to give us opportunities to increase our trust.

We also can't miss the fact that it is Moses who gives the directive to the Israelites about the manna. Looking back, we realize it is another form of the lesson he learned in Exodus 3. Moses discovered then the truth he must now pass on: God wants us to live in the present with our faith. Moses learned this lesson at the burning bush when he was denied future assurance for confronting Pharaoh; here he is called to teach the Israelites the same lesson—to stay with God in the now. In this we observe that the faith lessons we learn are not just for ourselves.

Whether our need is assurance or provision, tomorrow's need can drive us to fear and clinging today. Sometimes we even make choices to grab on to dead things because we are afraid to let go. Israelites who ignored Moses's warning found their manna filled with maggots the next morning. God's provision was designed not to last beyond a single day. Here we see a stark lesson in what happens when we live by fear—the thing we cling to is never as good as what God has; we just have to let go in order to receive it. But what we have is something we can *see*, and being willing to trade it for what we *can't* see is what God teaches us about faith in this passage. Whether or not we can do this is determined by the measure of our trust.

> Whether our need is assurance or provision, tomorrow's need can drive us to fear and clinging today.

How often we settle for what is in front of us when the desperation is great—whether it's a relationship, a job, or the promise of success. The temptation to grab at what is there and hold on to it is immense—even when you know that what is in front of you is not what is best. Franciscan priest and author Richard Rohr says, "To stay in God's hands, to trust, means that . . . I have to hold . . . a degree of uncertainty, fear, and tension."* The practice of uncertainty is what God gives the Israelites, and God extends this practice to us with each opportunity to trust. Each time we are willing to put our faith in God's provision, our faith grows, and when we experience the way God comes through, we build confidence for the next time we are called to take the risk.

Moses gives an instruction about the manna that we don't want to miss: "Everyone is to gather as much as they need" (Exodus 16:16). This instruction applies to God's provision today, although many of us are used to keeping more than we need. When the opportunity for plenty is in front of us, it's hard to restrict ourselves because we don't know what tomorrow will bring. Moses's directive not only helped the Israelites grow in their faith, but it taught them to share their abundance—trusting that God would provide. Letting go of the manna was as important as waiting for it to teach them the life of faith God wanted them to have.

So often when God brings abundance, we see ourselves as owners rather than stewards. That's where the trouble begins and the clinging starts. We think we are entitled to what we've received, and having too much becomes a lifestyle; we forget that God's provision is involved in everything we have. Even things we think we've earned have come from God; they are gifts that are given to us to steward and share. Our ability to let go of them and give to others out of our abundance is the freedom God dreams for us. Our response to the invitation to hold things loosely is determined by our amount of faith.

God knows that when we have too much or too little, the trouble begins. Either we become tempted to hoard and collect, or we anxiously grasp and cling; neither is conducive to a life of trust. "Just enough," God says to us through Moses, and with that guideline, we build an ongoing faith. God wants to increase our trust so that we will be able to hold what God gives us with open hands.

*Richard Rohr, *Everything Belongs: The Gift of Contemplative Fear* (New York: Crossroad, 2003), 144.

This passage also prods us to wait in faith for what God has for us, rather than grabbing what we have or can see. What God has for us may not come in the timing or the way we planned it, but if we are willing to let go and trust, we will see God work in a greater way. Only when the stakes are high, and the need impossible, do we really experience God's miraculous provision. This verse invites us to hold what we have loosely so that we can experience God's provision every day.

REFLECTION

1. On a scale of 1 to 10, how much do you trust God for ongoing provision in your life? Have you ever staked your well-being on God, or do you tend to play it safe with your faith?

2. When you have been given financial provision that is more than your present need, what do you do with your money? Do you think more about how you will save or about how you will give?

3. What is the hardest thing for you to let go of right now in your life? How did God speak to you in this passage?

7

The Temptation
to Find Another God

When God isn't doing what we want Him to do, we may feel like we want to replace Him. But first we need to examine what having another god will do to our souls. Exodus 32 reveals that when we replace our allegiance to God with a lesser god who will serve us, we will lose the control that initially tempted us. We eventually end up bowing to the god we enlist.

In this passage, the Israelites have grown impatient. When we are in this state, we often make poor choices fueled by our immediate need. Frustrated by Moses's absence, the Israelites decided they could not live in the unknown any longer. They took control of their wait instead of submitting to God's timing, and this is where the problems start. Their request to Aaron is comedic and ironic—they ask him to make "gods to go before" them. Wanting to follow what you make is an obvious oxymoron, but it reveals how twisted their thinking has become. Their God has parted a sea, rescued them from slavery, and provided food in the wilderness. Now they want to abandon God for an idol because He isn't showing up in the timeline they wanted.

The Israelites "gathered around Aaron," illustrating the fact that our choices are fueled by our company. The voices you surround yourself with will be the voices that influence you, so paying attention to your community is an important spiritual choice. "As for this fellow Moses who brought us up out of Egypt, we don't know what has happened to him," the crowd concludes. "This fellow Moses" has been their rescuer, leader, and provider. He has been on the mountain confirming the covenant of the commandments that will light their way. But the Israelites allow their wait to fill them with doubt and skepticism instead of letting it increase their ability to be patient. This is the choice we have when we don't know where God is—we either hold on to what we know and trust or let our current circumstances dictate our belief. The Israelites let the voices who have given up on God steer their faith.

Think about what would have happened if the verse began this way instead: "When the people saw that Moses was so long in coming down from the mountain, *they gathered around and worshiped and remembered all that God did.*" Perhaps we would have a different story in this chapter, and the Israelites would be spared the destruction produced by their idolatry. God gives us freedom in the wait; our response to the wait is up to us. By holding on to our memory of what God has done in our past, we have the capacity to build the faith muscle we need to persevere. Because of the Israelites' choices in this passage, they will not get that opportunity.

Waiting is part of our spiritual growth, and only by waiting do we gain the ability to wait. This is a lesson our soul needs to thrive. If we cannot wait, we will fall prey to every immediate desire that crosses our path; and following these desires can ultimately derail our lives. The golden calf that results from the Israelites' demand brings heartbreak and devastation, which is the final result of every pursuit apart from God. One bad choice leads to another, and in Exodus 32:6, we see the revelry and chaos the golden calf has produced. In this chapter, right in the middle of receiving the law, we get our first glimpse of our inability to be saved by the law, for the Israelites have already proven their inadequacy to follow it. Grace would have to be introduced to make salvation the final word.

The difficulty of the wait we are called to is nothing compared with the consequences we endure when we cannot wait. Trusting that God has been there for us in the past and promises to be again helps us not to abandon Him—even when we don't know where He is. Reading Exodus 32:1, we witness the irony and humor of the reasoning that led the Israelites in their decisions. Perhaps we can pause in observing their choices and recognize the reasoning we do in the choices we make ourselves. When we make a decision based on the frustration we have let fester rather than on the truth we can look back at and know, we are headed for trouble. The choices we make *before* the choice to abandon God are good to ponder before making a decision with consequences that can't be undone.

This passage also speaks to the temptation to worship the things we create. The things we make are unable to sustain us, and the more of ourselves we give to them, the more likely we are to let them ruin our lives. Whether it's a substance, a bank account, or a golden calf, the thing we grab on to apart from God will ultimately take control of our lives. We may want to abandon God when we feel disappointed, but we will discover that allegiance to any other god ends up destroying our lives. And when we look back, we discover God's puzzling actions often give us exactly we need.

> The thing we grab on to apart from God will ultimately take control of our lives.

From this passage we see that God is not abandoning us when He is silent, and we need to trust in times of waiting. The alternative of trading our allegiance to something we can control ultimately brings heartbreak, but we have to resist the immediate appeal another god can bring. What holding on to God brings us is worth every doubt that waiting for God might cause us. And if we can stay faithful, any doubts are destroyed when we see the result of what our faith has produced.

REFLECTION

1. Have you ever been tempted to give up and stop waiting on God because of what He did or didn't do? If so, when?

2. What other "gods" have you been tempted to follow because of a need or desire in your life?

3. When have you felt weakest in your faith? What helps your faith be strengthened?

8

The *Buts* That Steer Our Faith

> ### NUMBERS 13:27-28
>
> *[The land] does flow with milk and honey! Here is its fruit. But the people who live there are powerful, and the cities are fortified and very large. We even saw descendants of Anak there.*

The story starts out so well: Twelve spies are sent to survey a land they've been told is already theirs. What should have been a mission of celebration, however, turns into a mission of defeat. The spies allow a lens of fear to grow the obstacles they see in front of them. When they come back, they report a gross exaggeration of what they have seen. Our perspective can determine the success or failure of our journey of faith.

The spies' report begins with an affirmation of exactly what they were told they would see. The problem isn't with the land itself—it is with the way they *see* it, and that is where their faith begins to destruct. Instead of keeping their eyes fixed on what the land offers them, or the strategy they need to get what is already theirs, they begin to focus on all the reasons they won't be able to do what God has called them to do. By letting their fear color their report, they spill their doubt on others.

Numbers 13:27–28 reveals that "But" is not a good way to begin a sentence when it comes to encouraging those around us about matters of faith.

The spies had been asked to explore the land, not make a judgment on it (see v. 2). They had *already been told* the land was theirs—all that was left for them to do was believe. The obstacles were to be reported for strategy purposes, not as reasons to abandon their mission. Whether they should get the land or not wasn't a question they were supposed to address. Their fear instigated the doubt that eventually called their whole mission into question.

We cannot conquer the land if we don't have the courage to go into the land. This is what the spies learn in this passage. What begins as a *but* eventually becomes a barrier, and we see how the spies' report evolves as their fear grows. The people start out as big and end up being giants; the land described as spacious now "devours those who live in it"; the normal-sized spies transform to looking "like grasshoppers in [their] own eyes" (v. 33). Those last four words give us all the information we need about how their faith got hijacked. Their perspective paralyzed them in their journey.

> What begins as a *but* eventually becomes a barrier.

So let's pause here and think about how their perspective was shaped. Moses's instructions are clear: "Go and look at the land. See how many people there are. Assess the trees and soil. Bring back some fruit" (see vv. 17–20). The people in the land are only part of what Moses asked the spies to look for, yet the people become the focus of the report. The fruit, soil, and land flowing with milk and honey get sandwiched into one small sentence. Then they move on with a paragraph description of every people group who stood in their way (see v. 29). They minimize the good and maximize the bad, and the land evolves to match their perspective. They end up describing a fantasy of what is actually there. By the time they finish their report, the obstacles have grown several times their original size.

The perspective shift these Israelites have ends up coloring the memory of what they saw. This is evident not only in their description of the land but in what they say about Egypt in the next chapter. After letting fear spread like wildfire through the community, the people shout out, "Wouldn't it be better for us to go back to Egypt?" (Exodus 14:3), inspiring Moses—understandably—to fall face down in front of the whole community. We can only imagine this great leader's distress as the community of faith dissolves into a community of fear. This report has driven them to want to go back to the safety of the slavery from which they have just been freed.

Fear moves us back to what we've known, even if what we've known is what we formerly longed to escape. When we are led by fear, we sometimes choose the misery of the predictable over the risk of the unpredictable, because *what we picture* about our future has become worse than what we had. Faith (or the lack of it) shapes our perspective, and our perspective often determines our course. It's not that positive thinking changes our circumstances or controls what happens to us. But the lens of fear can keep us from positioning ourselves to receive all that God has. Choosing the way we see things could be a bigger decision than we thought.

Fear spreads like fire, and once again we see the power of community in shaping our faith. Only Caleb stands firm in his resolve about the land, and he is outnumbered by the ten spies who shut him down. How different the story could have been if the community had rallied around Caleb rather than the doubt-filled spies. It's a testament to paying attention to which voices around us cause the doubt and fear that weaken our faith. What the spies believe ends up being what actually happens to them—and ten of them never receive what God intended them to have. In the end, only Joshua and Caleb enter the land, because they are the only ones who believe they can conquer it. Fear prevents the others from receiving the blessing God wanted them to have.

There will always be a measure of fear when we step out in faith, but we have a choice in which one we allow to grow. Our choice to focus on faith or on fear determines not only what we see—but what happens in our lives. This passage shouts to us to let the *but* increase our resolve to live by faith rather than diminish it. Things may look bad, *but* God is big enough to see us through.

REFLECTION

1. Has your fear ever stopped you from acting on something you felt God might be calling you to do? If so, what was it?

2. Are you more surrounded by voices of faith or doubt? How does your crowd affect your faith?

3. Would you say you have a perspective that is colored more by fear or faith? What could help you see more with a faith lens instead of a fear lens?

9

For Our Own Good

At first glance, the Ten Commandments in Deuteronomy 5 might be viewed as restrictive and limiting. But Deuteronomy 10:13 gives us a perspective into God's commandments that helps us see them in a different way. Moses tells the Israelites that observing the commandments is not primarily for God's approval, but *for their own good*. The freedom we think we'll find by escaping these boundaries is actually found by living within them. Looking at what life looks like when we ignore the commandments helps us see their good.

"You shall have no other gods before me," the first commandment states, and the second commandment clarifies what that means by forbidding idolatry. The debacle of the golden calf in Exodus 32 affirms the life-giving wisdom behind these two commands. When we put something in God's place, we eventually learn its power is unable to sustain us. While most of us are not tempted to worship a golden calf, we *are* tempted to worship bank accounts, relationships, and pleasures; and what starts out as a quest for satisfaction or fulfillment turns into a trap. The freedom we initially pursued becomes a need the replacement can't fulfill, leaving us empty and wanting.

> The freedom we think we'll find by escaping these boundaries is actually found by living within them.

The third commandment, about not misusing God's name, is the third boundary that keeps God where He needs to be. God is our Creator and our Sustainer, and cheapening His name is an inadvertent attempt to downgrade God from the throne He is to occupy. God wants to be God, and the first three commands call us to confirm and uphold His deity for our own good.

"Observe the Sabbath day" is our guideline for rest and worship, and without this rhythm, our souls grow thin. If we spend every day working and producing, and no time reflecting or resting, we become a shell of the person we were meant to be. We know we were made for rest because our bodies tell us that every night—our very lives reveal our limitations and needs. The Sabbath pause for reflection helps us make room to see our need for God. The more we are able to see ourselves as temporary, the more apt we are to reach for eternal things, and the Sabbath gives us this opportunity.

"Honor your father and your mother" seems like a command for small children, but as our parents age, we realize this call to honor never stops. Our well-being is tied to the way we love the people who brought us into the world. When parents make mistakes, honoring them may mean setting a boundary around their behavior so that you won't repeat it. But giving them love and respect brings freedom to the place in your heart they will always fill.

"You shall not murder" seems an obvious boundary most of us do not cross. But there are ways to kill a person without taking a life. Our words and actions breathe life or death into people every day, and the choices we make in relationships either enrich or destroy them. We were meant to live in harmony, and this command reminds us that in living graciously toward others we find peace in our hearts.

"You shall not commit adultery" is a boundary our culture has grown to ignore, as millions of people engage in affairs as a mark of freedom and choice. But the freedom you initially find becomes a harness, and the problem you sought to escape soon doubles. Whatever choice you make after an affair will involve pain; it's just a matter of choosing which pain to endure. What also becomes clear when you embark on an affair is that half of every relationship is you. Sometimes the part of the relationship you yearn to escape turns out to be you—and you take yourself into every relationship. Only in keeping your commitments do you become the best version of yourself and experience the joy and fulfillment a long-term relationship can bring.

"You shall not steal"—whether it's stealing someone's husband or wife, their money or reputation, our choices sometimes involve stealing in ways we do not realize. Hoarding and keeping more than we need can also be a form of stealing—as it may impact someone else's survival. This command invites us to the life of *enough*, and the peace that comes in recognizing that *enough* is what we need.

"You shall not give false testimony" is a command of health and freedom, for life lived in a lie becomes constricted and small. We live in fear of being found out, and often have to tell more lies to keep the original lie safe. Lying takes energy away from living— and this command invites us to live in the freedom that only truth can bring. Even when truth brings consequences, the immediate effects of confession will never be as bad as the long-term costs lies produce. Living and speaking the truth sets us free.

"You shall not covet" helps us keep our eyes on our own blessings rather than focus on the blessings of someone else. The more we look and imagine, the more wonderful other people's lives become, and social media is coveting's greatest ally. When we are too busy focusing on other lives, we stop noticing the good in our own, and our lives seem emptier than they actually are. Coveting is a sure way to a life of misery, because wanting another life is an exercise in futility. Following this commandment helps us stay focused on the task of living the one and only life we have.

A closer look at the commandments God gave Moses helps us see why he declared that they were "for our own good." We may no longer be under the law since Jesus came to fulfill it (see Matthew 5:17), but Jesus knew it contained guidelines to help us live out our faith. Knowing and living these commandments brings our faith into life.

REFLECTION

1. Which of the commandments described above speaks most to your life right now? Why?

2. Which commandments do you have the hardest time with? Do you think of God's commandments as restrictive and outdated or still relevant? Why?

3. Look at what Jesus says in Matthew 5:17. What connection (if any) do you see between God's commandments and the life Jesus offers us?

10

Not Turning
to the Right or Left

JOSHUA 1:7

Be strong and very courageous. Be careful to obey all the law my servant Moses gave you; do not turn from it to the right or to the left, that you may be successful wherever you go.

When I was growing up, I used to go the racetrack with my dad to watch the racehorses compete. I loved to see the horses all dressed up to match their jockeys, but the racehorses wore something around their eyes I had never seen. I was told that because horses can be distracted by activity in their peripheral vision, they wear blinders to keep their eyes focused on what is straight ahead. Without them, a jockey would not be able to keep his horse from being sidetracked by what is happening to the right or left. Blinders are essential for a horse to have the best chance at winning a race.

49

In doing some research on blinders, I found an article that said it may have been a preacher who invented them. He was leading his horse down some unfamiliar stairs when the horse suddenly stopped, and he couldn't get him to budge. When he realized it was because of what the horse saw, he covered part of the horse's vision, and then had no problem getting it to move. The blinders enabled the horse to keep moving in uncertainty.[*]

Besides wondering if this horse ever made it into this preacher's sermon series, I am struck by the parallel between this illustration and God's words to Joshua. God is encouraging him to wear spiritual blinders to help Joshua maintain the focus he will need. Only by keeping his eyes fixed on God will Joshua be able to minimize the obstacles and distractions that threaten his success. If he lets the obstacles around him into his focus, they will grow in their capacity to lure him off God's path. The same is true for us.

Joshua has seen what happens when the focus gets shifted, with the ten spies on their expedition in Numbers 13. He knows the success of his mission will be largely due to the focus he is able to retain. By keeping his eyes forward, he will see only the next step he needs to take. His spiritual blinders will keep him from looking at the size of the whole mission, which could overwhelm him with the scale of the task. Like a racehorse with blinders, Joshua will need to focus on the leg of the journey that is just ahead.

Though most of us are not called to conquer a land, we *are* called to conquer our fears. To do that, we need our own spiritual blinders to help us step out in faith. The more we focus on our faith, the smaller our fear grows; however, we may not ever get to the place where fear completely leaves us. When you gawk at your fears, they will distract you and ultimately derail you. Consider Peter when he walked on water toward Jesus; when he kept his eyes on Jesus, he was able to take a few miraculous steps (see

*David Sanderson, "Why Do Horses Wear Blinders?," Dallas Equestrian Center, June 25, 2014, http://www.dallasequestriancenter.com/why-do-horses-wear-blinders.

Matthew 14:30) But when he looked at what was around him, he immediately started to sink. Peter learned the lesson Joshua learns in this passage: Where you focus your eyes can make all the difference in your walk of faith.

Keeping your eyes in front of you doesn't just keep you from focusing on your fears; it also keeps you from seeing detours that can lure you off the path. Rabbit trails and shortcuts sometimes appear more fun and may seem easier than the path God has called you to take. There are times when you may feel limited by God's path and want a different—or more exciting—route. Although God works your detours into the journey, they can distract you from God's call. Your spiritual blinders keep you from taking other roads along the path God is unfolding for your life.

> The more we focus on our faith, the smaller our fear grows.

One way to put on spiritual blinders is to think of adjusting a camera lens. With your lens set at a wide angle, you capture many things in your photograph. When you zoom in, everything but the object you are focused on disappears from view. This is the focus you need to move forward in your trust.

With every step of faith you take, the more faith you will have as you move ahead. Spiritual blinders help you block out your distractions so that you are able to move forward on God's path. Every time you experience God's provision and power, you gain more confidence on the mission God has for you. Keeping your eyes focused on what God has in front of you allows you to move forward in faith.

REFLECTION

1. Where do you need blinders in your faith right now? Is there something you need to stop focusing on that is a distraction to your faith?

2. Have you ever experienced getting tripped up because you didn't keep your eyes focused on what was ahead? If so, when?

3. Where in your life do you need courage to step out? What stood out in this reflection to inspire you?

11

Too Much of You Is Not Enough of God

JUDGES 7:2

The Lord said to Gideon, "You have too many men. I cannot deliver Midian into their hands."

When God's angel pronounces Gideon a mighty warrior, he is hiding in a winepress, threshing wheat where the enemy will not see. When we first meet Gideon, his transformation seems to be a story of the underdog rising, but this verse reveals the real theme. Gideon's primary call is not to become more than he is; it is to grow a trust in God that is bigger than what he has now. The battle is going to be God's—and Gideon's faith will give God the chance to shine. As Gideon is given fewer and fewer men for what he believes the battle requires, he has to believe more and more in what God can do, and this will require more trust than heroism.

Before the angel pronounces Gideon a mighty warrior, he tells him, "The Lord is with you" (Judges 6:12). This is the one necessary stipulation for Gideon to evolve into what the angel proclaims. It's interesting to observe Gideon's initial response: "If the Lord is with us, why has all this happened to us?" (v. 13). Gideon assumes that God's presence is aligned with his circumstances, and at this point in the story, Gideon's circumstances don't look good. But Isaiah 7:14 says Jesus will be called Immanuel, revealing that God does not dwell in our circumstances; God may use our circumstances, but *Immanuel* means "God with us." This is what Gideon and the Israelites discover in this passage.

"You have too many men" sounds as though God is being illogical. Aren't too many men what you need when you are battling an enemy that is stronger than you? But God is asking Gideon to prepare by paring down his army rather than building it up. This provides another insight about faith: God wants everything about the battle to point to His glory. If Gideon is to showcase God's power in the battle, he will need to rely on nothing except God. The less there is of Gideon, the more God's power will be revealed. This battle is an all-or-nothing proposition that will require Gideon to stake his life on his faith.

The Lord works with Gideon to increase his faith before the battle, but the battle itself will be Gideon's true test. Faith is only built by experience, and the more we risk, the more faith we acquire. Gideon has received proof that the Lord will give him victory (see Judges 6:16–33); God even allows him to put out a fleece for added assurance (see vv. 36–40). But even with all his fleeces, Gideon discovers that it's only in stepping out in our weakness that we see God come through for us. The more fear or insecurity we have, the greater our opportunity to let God shine. Sometimes the very center of your fear will be the place God wants you to go. I discovered this personally when God started opening doors for me to be a speaker—because public speaking was my greatest fear. But I knew that if I said no to the opportunities presented me, fear would rule my faith. God wants us to have a faith that rules our fears, not a faith that is controlled by them. Our choices affect how big our faith becomes.

In our lives, "too many men" can represent our talents, our control, our success, or our methods—the crutches we lean on instead of God. But this story teaches us that our greatest stories happen when we lean on nothing but God. The stories God has for us are always greater than we can imagine, but we have to be willing to let go of the crutches we are holding on to in order to experience them. God says, "Can you trust me?" and our answer determines what we see. Our faith allows us to bear witness to all that God can do.

In the end, God pares down Gideon's army to three hundred, and Scripture is silent about what Gideon must have felt. I can't imagine the panic that might have threatened his heart and pulled on him to retreat. But whatever Gideon felt, he proceeded with what God asked of him. And we discover in Gideon's obedience, God has all that He needs. Ultimately, Gideon wins the battle without even drawing a sword, and God uses the noise of their battle cry to secure their enemy's defeat. Just as the angel proclaimed Gideon a warrior before he became one, the battle cry proclaims Gideon's victory before the victory unfolds—these two incidents give us another insight about the way God works. Believing what God says paves our way to the opportunity to watch God do it. You can trust that, whatever is before you, God can be relied upon to help you succeed.

> Our greatest stories happen when we lean on nothing but God.

After the battle, Gideon's reputation and leadership grow because he trusts God enough to step out and let God use him. It is Gideon's willingness to believe that enables him to become what God knows he can be. Believing is no easy task, as it often requires risk and upheaval for us to act on it. The fear of wondering what will happen if God *doesn't* come through can keep us from taking a risk. But when we experience God doing something through us that we never imagined possible, it changes our faith forever. Watching Gideon's relationship with God soar after this battle, we bear witness to this truth.

REFLECTION

1. Is there an area or concern in your life where you need to grow your trust in God? What is it?

2. Would you describe the way you live your faith as more of your strength and less of God's, or more of God's strength and less of yours? What is one step you could take to rely more on Him?

3. Is there anything you've avoided doing because you were afraid or felt inadequate? What might God be calling you to do right now with Gideon faith?

12

Hearing God's Voice

1 SAMUEL 3:10

The Lord came and stood there, calling as at the other times, "Samuel, Samuel!" Then Samuel said, "Speak, for your servant is listening."

When it happens, you might not know what to make of it. Whether through a sermon, a passage of Scripture, or a voice inside, you may feel that God has spoken to you. The volume goes up, and the words you hear (or read) seem as if they were meant just for you. But this passage about Samuel reveals that *hearing* God's voice is just the beginning of what it means to *listen* to God's voice. And the way we listen to God can make a difference in what we'll continue to hear.

When I was in seminary, one of my professors introduced me to the term *agogic moment*. He defined it as a moment when we are spoken to by something bigger than ourselves. As seminary students, we were learning to discern how God spoke, and this phrase described it in a way that made sense. An agogic moment can happen when you're listening to a preacher's voice, talking to a friend, or reading a sentence in a book. But in that moment, you suddenly feel like something you hear or see was meant just for you. The agogic moment can only be initiated by God, and its effect is determined by the person who experiences it. If the moment is ignored or passed off, it will not have its intended effect. Perhaps that is one way to understand what is going on in this chapter.

God speaks repeatedly to Samuel (see 1 Samuel 3:4–8), but because Samuel doesn't recognize God's voice, the connection is not made. When Eli realizes God is talking to Samuel, he gives him words to say to make the connection. With the words of response in this verse, Samuel shows that he finally is ready to hear what God has to say.

"Speak, for your servant is listening," Samuel says; and it is in this posture that we are best prepared to not only hear but listen. Eli can tell by Samuel's repeated experience that he is hearing God's voice, and he instructs Samuel how to respond the next time God speaks to him. From Eli's help, we can observe that God's voice is best interpreted in community. Otherwise, we are left to interpret the voice ourselves, which is never the surest way to know what God says. If you hear a voice of hopelessness, ridicule, or condemnation, it is likely *not* God's voice, and it is important to find someone who can help you distinguish it. If God is speaking to you about a sin, or about a change or movement in your life, checking with other believers who know you will help you determine whether the voice seems right. Eli is able to help Samuel recognize God's voice and then be receptive for what God has to say.

We cannot manufacture an agogic moment, but we can prepare people for it. This is what Eli does when he helps Samuel know how to respond. By guiding people to be present and attentive to what they see and hear, we can help people be more likely to experience God's voice; and when people think they hear it, we can help them discern what they hear. This is what Eli does for Samuel in this passage.

By coming alongside Samuel in his agogic moment, Eli is able to let him know how to hear the words God has for him. When Samuel heeds Eli's advice, he opens himself to what God has to say. Samuel positions himself to hear from God by using the words that Eli has given him. "Speak, for your servant is listening" is a very different posture than "Listen to me, God, while I tell you what to do." When we ask God to speak, we need to be prepared to do what God says. Instead of approaching God as being there to serve us, we are to be ready to serve God. With this attitude, we are ready to hear and act on what God says.

It is ironic that what God says to Samuel is really for Eli. It is a dark time in Israel's history, as indicated in 1 Samuel 3:1: "In those days the word of the Lord was rare; there were not many visions." Our receptivity has a lot to do with how much God speaks, and it seems God's voice has grown faint because the people of that time aren't interested in what God has to say. Eli's sons have not carried on their father's priesthood well, and God has brought Samuel in to clean house and better represent Him. The news Samuel hears from God is bad news for Eli's sons, so Samuel is afraid to tell Eli. But Eli shows his receptivity to God by his openness to hear Samuel's words no matter what those words are. Unfortunately for Eli, God declares there will be no future for his family's priesthood since his own receptivity has not been carried on through his sons.

> When we ask God to speak, we need to be prepared to do what God says.

"Speak, for your servant is listening" is a phrase that will mark Samuel's ministry for the rest of his life. A giant of the Old Testament, Samuel will be called to appoint Israel's first king (Saul), condemn that king when he goes astray, and ultimately choose the next king, who will be remembered as a man after God's own heart. When Samuel appoints David, the least likely pick from the line of Jesse's sons, it is only by having an ear trained to listen to God that Samuel is able to choose him—and David becomes the greatest king to occupy Israel's throne. Samuel knows God's voice intimately, and that leads him to hear from God throughout his life. The same applies to us today: The more we respond to God's voice, the more confident we become in recognizing it.

REFLECTION

1. Would you call yourself more of a hearer of God's Word or a listener of God's Word? Why?

2. Have you had an "agogic moment" in your faith journey? What was your response to it?

3. Whom in your life can you ask to help you discern God's voice?

13

The Decisions
before the Decision

2 SAMUEL 11:1

In the spring, at the time when kings go off to war, David sent Joab out with the king's men and the whole Israelite army.

People who don't even read the Bible are familiar with the story of David and Bathsheba. This chapter in David's life shows us a vivid illustration of how quickly temptation can derail us in our faith. But the beginning of 2 Samuel 11 shows us that falling into temptation does not happen with a single decision. It happens because of all the decisions *before* that decision that weaken our resolve. One small decision can end up affecting our entire course.

With an opening that says, "At the time when kings go off to war," we would expect the sentence to finish with "King David led his men into battle." But it is in the middle of this sentence that we see David's first bad step. We don't know why David sends Joab with his army, but we can speculate. Maybe he is exhausted from his previous battle (see 2 Samuel 10:18) and knows Joab is a strong enough leader to go in his place. Maybe he has business to attend to at the palace and feels he cannot go. But whatever leads David to decide not to take his place with his men ultimately sets the stage for his downfall. In this seemingly small decision, he makes space for the temptation that will derail his course.

With each poor choice we make, the momentum to go in the wrong direction picks up, and as temptation moves forward, our desire becomes harder to subdue. The fall into temptation is easier to interrupt in the earlier stages, so it's the earlier decisions we need to amend in order to set ourselves on the better course. Whether it's a person we need to avoid, an internet site we need to block, a sip we need to refrain from, or an event we need to decline, these small decisions set us on a path that can determine our fate. Once we position ourselves in a place we shouldn't be, we are more likely to proceed with something we shouldn't do. David discovered this truth after he made the seemingly inconsequential decision not to leave home.

> Once we position ourselves in a place we shouldn't be, we are more likely to proceed with something we shouldn't do.

Because I was single until my late forties, I had many pre-decisions to contend with in my own life. In my friendships with married men, initial decisions paved the way for how the friendships would evolve. When I made poor early decisions, even ones that appeared harmless, some friendships had to end for protection. Paying attention to early decisions prevents more difficult decisions from having to be made later. In this passage, David discovers this truth.

Bored and listless after waking from his nap, David apparently has too little to do. Empty room in our schedule is not the best setup for confronting temptation. As David makes his way up to his roof to stroll, it's important to note some things from that time in Israel's history: Evening was normally the time people took baths, to avoid the heat; outdoor bathing, often in an enclosed courtyard, was a common practice because they did not have indoor plumbing; and the king's roof would have been the highest position in the city. So taking a stroll at this hour is another bad choice David makes.

From the roof stroll forward, David's decisions move fast, and they all happen in the next three verses. David sees, inquires, ignores the answer, then proceeds—and in this rapid progression, we see how temptation takes its course. David's unbridled desire makes each successive choice hard to stop, even when warning signs flash before him. "Is this not Bathsheba, the daughter of Eliam, the wife of Uriah the Hittite?" the messenger prods (v. 3 NASB), and David's silence tells us all we need to know. Ultimately the messenger's warning is ignored, and not even the knowledge that Bathsheba is married to one of his soldiers can stop him. David charges forward despite the warnings, and when Bathsheba becomes pregnant, he gets a whole new problem to solve. At this point we may wonder if David wishes he had gone to war.

The decisions after we fall are limited because we can't undo what has already been done. This makes the decisions *before* temptation the place to focus on first. By slowing down and looking closely at what sets up our decision to proceed, we may find wisdom for future decisions before it's too late. God's grace prevails— but pain is the fallout of every bad choice.

What we witness in this heartbreaking chapter in David's life is that one bad decision breeds another. Only when we have the courage to make a good decision can we turn the story around. The later that decision comes, the more pain we endure and inflict on others. David discovered that after he finally turned around to see all the tragedy he left in his wake. With a hero fallen and a child lost, the words of Psalm 51 lead us to assume David regretted his one-night decision. Looking at what David could have done differently *before* that decision gives us the wisdom we need for avoiding his fate.

REFLECTION

1. Think of a temptation that you succumbed to in your life. Now reflect on all the decisions you made *before* you succumbed. Is there any decision you could have made differently that would have affected the outcome?

2. Is there anything you know you should be acting upon but are not? How is what you are not doing setting you up for future decisions?

3. Is there a current circumstance in your life about which you need to think through the decisions you are making and where they may lead? Is there someone you could talk to about this for support?

14

Elijah's School of Faith

1 KINGS 17:3-4

Leave here, turn eastward and hide in the Kerith Ravine, east of the Jordan. You will drink from the brook, and I have directed the ravens to supply you with food there.

There is no Old Testament figure apart from Moses who towers higher than Elijah. His presence in the transfiguration with Jesus confirms his prominence (see Mark 9:4). This passage in 1 Kings reveals how the great faith that marked Elijah's life begins in a ravine where he is alone with some ravens. Before Elijah's public showdown with the gods, God takes him on a personal journey to grow his faith. It seems God wants Elijah to be able to speak to others with the conviction of experience.

In 1 Kings 17:1, the first words out of Elijah's mouth exhibit a bullish faith. But to be able to stand in the strength of his faith in a culture where other gods are worshiped, Elijah will need the personal experience of watching God's faithfulness himself. However, Elijah has to be willing to do what God asks him to do in order to experience it. "Leave here, turn eastward and hide in the Kerith Ravine," God says, and it may be helpful to consider how strange God's request actually is. Most prophets in the Old Testament were called to *go* to begin their ministry, but in Elijah's case, he is called to *leave*. The first chapter of ministry God has planned for Elijah will be for Elijah alone. This verse reveals that our relationship with God is of primary importance to how our ministry unfolds.

Elijah will one day need to call on God to perform a huge public miracle. So God wants Elijah to experience a personal miracle in order to be emboldened for the future task. It is of particular importance that the miracle God chooses is one that Elijah has to depend on for survival. This isn't a miracle Elijah will witness from afar, but one he will participate in by risking his life. The risk Elijah takes by going to the ravine alone without food brings the dependence God wants. The bigger our need is, the more faith we end up with when we watch God come through.

> The bigger our need is, the more faith we end up with when we watch God come through.

In that repeated action of watching the ravens bring his food, Elijah develops the faith muscle he needs for what is ahead. The display of God's sovereignty in having the ravens feed Elijah is purely for Elijah's benefit; and because it is bread and meat (not water and wafers), Elijah basks daily in God's grace. God could have provided for Elijah in other ways, but bringing food for him this way reveals God's power over nature. This is information Elijah will one day need in the ministry that awaits him. Watching God use the birds as food carriers, Elijah now knows God is capable of doing anything he asks.

The greater the risk God requires to see the miracle, the greater effect the miracle has on our faith. The more dependent we are on

God to come through—whether facing a task we are terrified to do or a habit we need to overcome—the more we witness God's capacity. If God had not come through in feeding Elijah, his life would have ended in that ravine. Instead, his spiritual life was ignited. From this point forward, Elijah's prophetic ministry will carry a reputation unmatched in Israel's history.

After Elijah's miraculous episode with the ravens, he is sent to the house of a widow who has been commanded to feed him. When Elijah arrives at the widow's house, she is about to eat her last meal and die—not exactly the greeting he pictured. But because of his time with the ravens, he is able to take the next step of trust for how God will handle the situation. With the provision he boldly asks for, he is able to feed this woman with the food that God supplies. In this progression of faith, we see a picture of how ministry begins.

When we are fueled in our own faith, we are equipped to fuel others; but often we neglect the former in our excitement to do God's work. Elijah's story affirms the importance of allowing God to fuel our own faith so that we then bring a faith to others based on what we've personally seen God do. The command to *leave* is as important as the command to *go* in Elijah's ministry—and Elijah hears *go* only after he has been fed. Without the experience of letting God fill him, there would have been less of God *in* him to do God's work.

We also learn from Elijah that being filled in our own faith isn't a one-time occurrence. The showdown with the prophets of Baal (see ch. 18) leaves him feeling devastated and empty, and he loses perspective in his faith. Elijah needs to be reminded of who God is so that he can remember what God has done; another experience of being filled and fed will recover him (see ch. 19). The lesson Elijah learns in 1 Kings 17:3–4 is a lesson that will follow him throughout his life.

Just as a car needs regular refueling, being filled in our own faith is both necessary and continual. Without it, our faith will shrink up, fade, or die. We cannot continue to live what we do not personally know, and God wants our faith to be emboldened. This can only happen with the experience of trusting God with something so big, we can't help but grow as we watch God come through. And our faith grows with us.

REFLECTION

1. Think about a big need that you had to rely on God to provide. How did His provision impact your relationship with Him (or your faith)?

2. Has God ever called you to learn a lesson that you were going to eventually pass on to others? Is God doing anything like that in your life right now?

3. Do you think there is a correlation between the size of your need and the amount your faith grows? On a scale of 1 to 10, how big is your faith? How big do you want it to be?

15

The Courage to Pray
for the Bigger Story

1 CHRONICLES 17:23

And now, Lord, let the promise you have made concerning your servant and his house be established forever.

You can't have a bad story in your book about someone great and not include a good story. There are many stories in David's life besides his encounter with Bathsheba that give us a fuller perspective of the man he was. Here in this prayer we see David's humble heart displayed—and how he sees himself as a servant in God's greater story. He knows that God's story has gone on before him and will continue after he is gone. His words of humility and acceptance give us words to pray when God unveils a plan that will live beyond us.

Part of our development—both socially and spiritually—is to recognize we are part of a bigger story. As babies, we think we are the center of our world, and things don't exist when they leave our sight. Gradually, we realize things happen when we are not there, and our perspective shifts. Spiritually, we develop the same way, and part of our maturity is to recognize we are not the center of our story, but part of God's bigger story. Things have happened before us and they will continue to happen after us. Knowing we are a part of what God is unfolding helps us have perspective in the way we live our lives.

In 1 Chronicles 17, God speaks to David about building a temple. David has waited for this his whole life—it will be a place for Israel to finally worship God in a stable homeland where they will not be disturbed (see v. 9). Then come the details: "I will raise up your offspring. . . . He is the one who will build a house for me" (vv. 11–12). David will never see this promise fulfilled, for it will be his son who will see this greatness come to pass.

"Let the promise you have made . . . be established forever," David says, and we can learn from this affirmation. His words are of particular importance as we consider the way we accept the plans God has for us. First David affirms God's plan, without asking God to speed up the timing or change it—although we cannot help but think he wishes it would unfold sooner. He understands that God's perspective is much broader than his, and for whatever reason, this promise will be fulfilled not by him, but by his son. David's affirmation reflects that his part on earth is God's to write, and he submits to that knowledge without reservation. He knows there is a greater story being written around him, and with joy and acceptance, he affirms his part.

Pausing here, we can consider how we feel about our role in God's story. We may have things we wish God would do in our timing, but they could be part of a future unfolding that is much bigger than us. Submitting to the part we play, and the timing we've been given to play it, is one of the greatest ways we can say yes to God. David shows us how to defer to God's bigger plan while we humbly play our part.

I remember reading a story in Charles Colson's book *Loving God* about a man named Boris Kornfeld. He was a doctor who was taken to serve in a Soviet labor camp, where he gave his life to Christ. Aware that his time might be limited, Kornfeld shared his faith with a young patient who had intestinal cancer. This patient was so impressed by Kornfeld's conviction that he hung on every word he said and became convinced himself. After Boris Kornfeld was killed, that patient gave his life to Christ. He went on to become one of the greatest Russian authors of all time, and when he won the Nobel Prize in Literature, Alexander Solzhenitsyn became a name that was known worldwide. But it was an unknown doctor named Boris Kornfeld who set that famous author on his path.[*]

I believe the story of Boris Kornfeld is a perfect illustration of the books we will one day read in heaven. Instead of reading about Mother Teresa or Billy Graham, we may read books about the unnamed people around them who brought them to faith. This is the perspective that God gives us as we pull back to see the bigger view—and we are emboldened to take whatever place we have in God's story. However big or small our part is, we are merely a thread of what God is doing in our midst.

There is a side note of sacrifice in this passage that we should notice. Having God's perspective means we are willing to *not* see what we want to see or have what we want to have as God's story unfolds. Our no in God's story may mean someone else's yes, and our willingness to bear that no may include sacrifice. Jesus taught us this truth when the no He was willing to bear in the garden of Gethsemane became God's yes for all of us. David upholds this same truth when he affirms that the task of building a temple will be deferred to his son; and he establishes the focal

> Our no in God's story may mean someone else's yes.

*Charles Colson, *Loving God* (Grand Rapids, MI: Zondervan, 1996), 27–33.

point of his story with these words: "Do as you promised . . . that your name will be great forever" (vv. 23–24).

REFLECTION

1. Think of some situations you have experienced where your role was less significant than you wanted. How does this story of David encourage you about how you have been used in a bigger story?

2. Are there any areas in your life where you need to take the focus off yourself and submit to the bigger plan of God's glory?

3. In what roles in your life are you contributing to someone else's story (a parent's, spouse's, employee's, etc.)? Is there anything you are motivated to do differently in order to support someone else better than you are?

16

The Story within the Story

ESTHER 4:14

*If you remain silent at this time, relief and deliverance for the Jews will arise from another place.
. . . Who knows but that you have come to your royal position for such a time as this?*

The unique trait of the book of Esther is that it is the one book in the Bible that doesn't ever mention God's name. Instead, much as in life, God's presence is revealed in the actions and decisions of the people in the book. Esther's story illustrates that there is always more going on than we can see, and the story we are in could have a different purpose from what we think. The more visible God's purpose becomes, the more we find ourselves presented with a choice in how we will respond.

When Esther's story begins, it almost feels like an episode of *The Bachelor*. The Persian king has deposed his queen, so he brings in all the beautiful maidens of the land for a chance to win his heart. Esther is described as "very beautiful and lovely" (Esther 2:7 NLT), so she is swept up in this contest, and after being brought to the palace, she stands out from the other maidens and ultimately wins the king's heart. Most movies roll the credits at this point, leaving us with two words: *THE END.* From God's perspective, however, Esther's story has just begun.

After she becomes queen, Esther finds out that the king's advisor has plotted to have the Jews obliterated. The king has signed the edict that will carry out the advisor's plan, not fully aware of what he has decreed. It is at this point that Esther's cousin Mordecai challenges Esther with the responsibility she has been given with her position. Because she has been placed in the palace, she is the only one in a position to intervene. Suddenly, Esther realizes there is a whole different story going on around her than she initially saw, and this story contains a bigger purpose for her than she imagined. What she does next will determine the role she plays.

In Esther 4:11, Esther lays out in detail why she feels can't do what Mordecai asks. Her response comes from how she views her limitations as queen, and the enormity of the risk Mordecai is asking her to take. Instead of getting Mordecai's sympathy, however, she is confronted by his strong challenge. The fear she feels moving forward in her story is put in the context of what *not* moving forward will mean. Mordecai reminds Esther that she is here "for such a time as this," but the words he says *before* that phrase are the words we should focus on first. "If you remain silent at this time, relief and deliverance for the Jews will arise from another place," Mordecai warns Esther. Mordecai turns Esther's fear of moving forward into the greater fear of what she'll miss if she *doesn't* do what she has been brought here to do.

Mordecai's words to Esther reveal that she is *already taking part* in this other story. Her decision to speak or remain silent will simply define the part she will play. If she remains silent, her part will be safe and small; if she decides to speak up, it will be risky and big. The fear Esther has to face is that she cannot see how it will all turn out. Esther is invited to pull back on her life and see that everything she has been given—her beauty, her triumph, her position in the palace—was given to her for a purpose, for what she will do in this moment. Her response to Mordecai's challenge will be the turning point of her life. If she remains silent, Mordecai warns her, the more significant story will go on without her. Esther may move forward in her smaller story, but it will never carry the weight of what she does here. Esther stands at the crossroads where all of us stand in our faith.

Perhaps there is a word from Mordecai about perspective of ownership that can also speak to us. To move forward with this sacrifice, Esther will have to see her beauty as given to her rather than crafted, her victory as orchestrated instead of earned. From this perspective she will see Mordecai's call as something God has created her to do. With this same perspective we can look at what we've been given and consider Mordecai's challenge. If we never give God the things we have, we will never know what God could have done with them. We see only as much of His power as our sacrifice and vision allow.

> If we never give God the things we have, we will never know what God could have done with them.

Faith always increases as it is acted on, and in Esther's decision to move forward, her confidence grows. Calling for a fast (see v. 16), the closest indication of prayer we see in this story, she has clearly settled on what she must do. The same strong language that betrayed her fear in verse 11 now becomes language to build her determination; and with each word she says, her resolve and fortitude increase. The fear that she initially had becomes incidental to the direction she must take. Her words at the end of verse 16 indicate how strong her determination has become: "If I perish, I perish."

In this moment, Esther's identity shifts from queen to deliverer. She has chosen to give what she has back to God and sacrifice her gifts and privileges so that others will find relief. In Esther's call, we find our own.

REFLECTION

1. Do you look for God's purpose in your circumstances, or do you focus only on the circumstances themselves? How does Esther's story challenge you?

2. Have you ever looked back on a situation and seen how God worked in a different way from what you expected? If so, when?

3. Consider the gifts, talents, and position that God has given you. How can you begin to see the bigger role God has for you in His story? What is one step you can take to lean in to that bigger role?

17

God's Affection in Our Trials

> ## JOB 1:8
>
> *Have you considered my servant Job? There is no one on earth like him; he is blameless and upright, a man who fears God and shuns evil.*

Why is God allowing me to suffer? we cry, searching for answers as to why something is—or is not—happening in our life. The problem of pain can create spiritual distance between us and God and even cause some believers to abandon their faith. The first chapter of Job, however, demonstrates the remarkable possibility that God's allowing our suffering may be a sign of God's affection. It may also be evidence that we have a God who believes in us more than we believe in ourselves.

Before calamity hits Job, we are privy to a conversation that Job knows nothing about. Satan is roaming the earth, presumably looking for someone to tempt, and it is God who initiates the conversation. "Have you considered my servant Job?" God says, and like a proud parent showing off his kids, God presents Job as the child He is currently admiring. Extolling Job's qualities, God describes Job as someone who will put Satan's condemnation of humanity to the greatest test. In laying Job out like a trophy, God puts so much confidence in Job that we are not surprised at Satan's next taunt. With everything Job has been given, Satan insists that Job's affection is conditional because of all that Job has. "Strike everything he has," Satan snarls, "and he will surely curse you to your face" (v. 11). Satan knows that when those things are stripped away, Job will have no reason other than his commitment to God to hold on to his faith. With this challenge, Job's descent into pain is conditionally approved.

Let's pause to consider the options. God could walk away from Satan's challenge, but this could look as though God doubts whether Job is really the man He just described to Satan. Or God can bank on Job and stake His reputation on Job's response. God stands on His belief in Job even before Job has a chance to live up to it. It is out of God's confidence in Job, not His condemnation of him, that Job's suffering is allowed.

> God believes in us enough to move our faith beyond the things He gives us—and to see His favor in what He asks from us instead.

When we suffer, it is an opportunity to see that God believes in us enough to move our faith beyond the things He gives us—and to see His favor in what He asks from us instead. Our sufferings change and expand us, and we learn more about God, ourselves, and others in suffering than at any other time. The more we allow ourselves to be stretched in suffering, the more God's heart for our lives can be revealed.

It is important to note that God doesn't allow Job's catastrophes merely to prove Satan wrong and "beat" him. God ultimately allows Job's catastrophes because He wants to move Job into a deeper faith. God is wooing Job through his suffering into a deeper understanding of who He is—and that His love stands apart from Job's circumstances. God is *with* Job in his circumstances, and Job will discover that in the end. It is also important to see that while Job's suffering may be allowed by God, his suffering is not caused by God. Satan is the source of Job's suffering, and God takes His place on Job's side as he receives his blows. This is the first time in Scripture that we see a vivid illustration of God separating himself from what is happening *to* us and taking His place beside us.

God does not instigate Job's pain; God is Job's cheerleader through it. Pronouncing him faithful and upright, God proclaims in advance that He believes Job will bear up under this suffering. By telling Satan that Job *fears God and shuns evil*, God is declaring that his faith will endure, and Job will not walk away. God's confidence in Job is apparent before we as the reader know how Job will respond to this trial. Here we get a glimpse of what God may feel in our trials with the confidence He has for us.

The exhortations of Job's friends in the chapters that follow reveal that suffering up to this point has been viewed as punishment. Whatever Job or his family has done, the belief is that if Job corrects it, the suffering will cease. In verse 8, we see for the first time that our circumstances may have nothing to do with our actions. While our actions can incur suffering, there are reasons for our suffering that are beyond our understanding or reach. God uses suffering to strengthen our commitment to Him because God knows we can get through it with Him. Only after we've made it through suffering do we see what suffering does in enlarging our hearts.

Job loses all that God has given him, but Job's devotion ultimately deepens. This is perhaps the greatest mystery when it comes to growing our faith. Only when things are stripped away do we truly recognize God's sufficiency. Witnessing how Job's relationship with God grows through his devastation helps us see God's hope for us.

When God allows us to suffer, not only does our faith grow, but our compassion is stretched. The fact that Job is called upon to pray for his friends at the end of the book reveals how God has already begun to use this in his life (see Job 42:10). Job has gained an understanding his friends' theology lacks, and this will allow him to be used more profoundly to minister to others. This is the gift suffering gives us, although it may feel at first like God has turned His back on us. Through Job 1, we learn that God may be holding us up to stake His claim on our faith. With that understanding to strengthen us, we have more courage to bear up under our sufferings. We see in Job's story the honor it may possibly be.

REFLECTION

1. If God suddenly took away all the things in your life that you consider good, would your love for God change? How?

2. Have you had a time of suffering in your life? How did it impact your faith? Did you feel it was a punishment from God?

3. Does the idea that suffering can actually be a sign of God's favor and trust cause you to see your suffering differently?

18

Seeing Our Life in Context

JOB 42:3

Surely I spoke of things I did not understand,
things too wonderful for me to know.

Imagine if you discovered one day that you were always looking through the lens of a microscope. Everything you saw was actually just a miniscule, close-up particle of what really was. Then one day, someone pulled the microscope away and showed you what you were seeing in the context of the bigger picture. The view you thought was the whole picture turned out to be just a tiny section of the world you now see. In that moment, you would know how Job felt when God gave him a broader view of his sufferings. Like Job, your need for answers would change with the knowledge of context that you now had.

In this verse, there is a remarkable shift in Job's perspective about his sufferings. After spending many chapters questioning God, he is suddenly moved to repentance because of what he has seen. God never directly answers Job's questions about his suffering; instead, God pulls back Job's microscope and reveals how big the world is around him. After seeing his life in this context, Job's demand for God to explain his sufferings no longer becomes his focus. His eyes have been shifted from the injustice of his pain to the magnitude of God.

Job's questioning of God ceases, and he is now ready to answer the question God has asked him: "Who is this that obscures my plans with words without knowledge?" (Job 38:2). With his humble response, Job realizes the limited view he has had on the things that have happened to him. Though his new perspective does not change the difficulty of his suffering, his pain is now understood in the context of broader things. Watching the intricacy of how things fit together in the universe, Job sees that his life is part of a bigger story. He recognizes that his pain may reach out and connect with others in a way he doesn't know now but will someday see.

When we see our sufferings in a broader context, it helps us understand the pain we go through differently. When Job says, "I spoke of things . . . too wonderful for me to know," he is expressing newfound hope from what God has revealed. This hope has assured Job that the suffering he went through was not pointless or arbitrary, but part of something bigger. The fact that millions of people (including you reading this now) are helped by Job's story affirms that Job's hope was right. Perhaps that gives you hope in your suffering that God will one day use it for a bigger purpose. It doesn't take the pain away, but it may give you a new perseverance to endure it for what that pain will bring. Like a mom in childbirth, there is a greater and different understanding of your pain when you see a bigger picture around it. You know your pain may lead to something wonderful that you will one day see.

The bigger picture of suffering includes not only what happens around you but what is happening in you. In Job's new understanding of God, we see how pain has ultimately deepened and changed his faith. By getting a glimpse of the largeness of God's creation, he recognizes there are many dimensions to his life that he can't understand from his limited vision. This gives him a new submission to how God works things together that increases his trust. Knowing God can do all things, Job places the reason for his pain into the context of God's greater purpose. What God saw in Job at the beginning of the book has now come to fruition with Job's new eyes.

Throughout the book of Job, we are invited to wrestle with many of the great questions we have about suffering. Note, however, that the book ends with no more answers about suffering than when it began. When the microscope is pulled back, Job doesn't learn more about why people suffer. His questions about his suffering have disappeared against the backdrop of the greater knowledge he now has of God. Job is no longer caught up in the *why* of his suffering because he has been overwhelmed by the *who* behind it. His repentant attitude reveals the perspective shift that has expanded his faith.

Once the microscope is pulled away, we see our life differently when we go back to our immediate circumstances. The details that previously held our focus now carry new and different meaning because of what we have seen. Once we've seen through God's eyes, our eyes are never the same.

> Once we've seen through God's eyes, our eyes are never the same.

At the end of the book, Job's sores disappear, his wealth is restored, and he gains back double what he had. Yet the sorrow of his losses will be carried from this point forward in his heart. New children bring new joy, but the hole of grief for his former children will endure inside him. He will now learn to hold the goodness of life with what his losses have taught him, and his heart will grow with the perspective he has gained. It seems the real story about Job is not what he gained or lost, but what happened inside of him. The widening of Job's perspective has given him a bigger faith with a greater trust in a greater God. Ultimately, this is God's desire for all of us.

REFLECTION

1. When you look at the pain you've been through in light of the bigger picture of people around you, how might God use it?

2. Have you ever had an experience of going through a trial and then helping someone go through the same trial? If so, what happened?

3. How does seeing the big picture affect the way you see your individual story? Do you feel that your perspective has an impact on the way you view your circumstances? If so, how?

19

A Weaned Faith

PSALM 131:2

I am like a weaned child with its mother; like a weaned child I am content.

If you have ever been present when a child is weaned, you know the experience can be a little unsettling. While a mother resists satisfying her baby's cry, she is actually loving her child into growth. Though it may be frightening to think about, imagine if you never went through this growth step in your maturity. (That is one scary image.) Your mother spared you that awkwardness by going through the pain of doing what she had to do. It was the first of many times you were declined in your desires so that you could become the person you are right now. From parenting, we understand that all of us have had something we wanted withheld by someone who loves us for the sake of our growth. According to this little psalm, that may be one way to understand how spiritual growth is with God.

Psalm 131 begins with David in a humbled state—presumably due to something that has happened or not happened in his life. David says that God is doing "things too wonderful" for him to know, echoing Job's words as he reflects an understanding that there is a bigger picture happening around his life. David describes himself as a weaned child, repeating the phrase but offering two different angles on the meaning. The first time he says he is "like a weaned child with its mother"; the second time he says, "Like a weaned child I am content." In the first phrase, he describes himself positioned right next to the source of his security and blessing. In the next phrase, he has learned to settle apart from his security and blessing, still knowing he is loved. In David's description, we see a perfect picture of what God desires for our faith.

When we first become believers, we are focused on the things we want God to do for us, and when God answers our prayers, our hearts are full of love. Without being aware of it, our love can become conditional on the blessings God fulfills for us. If we stay in this stage in our faith, we may never see the bigger plans that God has for our lives.

Inherent to the process of our spiritual weaning, however, is pain. We have desires that God may not give us in the time or way we want, and sometimes we feel a yearning ache. In my own life, two of those desires were marriage and motherhood. When I walked down the aisle at forty-nine, I was presented on my wedding day with a six-year-old stepson, whom I have had the joy and privilege to raise. My prayer for motherhood was not fulfilled the way I had prayed it, but opening my heart to how God would answer that prayer helped me welcome what God had for me. In time, I was able to see my small prayer answered in light of a bigger prayer that involved more people and more needs.

When we *still and quiet our soul* regarding our unanswered prayers, we often see that God's answers are bigger than the prayers we gave Him. They are "things too wonderful" for us to understand because they involve more people and circumstances than we could originally see. As our faith matures, we give God more editing power in our prayers. We know there are reasons God withholds from us, and a weaned faith allows us to trust Him as we present our requests, God may have something better in mind, and it may involve different circumstances or timing. Our willingness to wait for God to answer is our sacrifice as we believe He is doing things we can't imagine. Waiting to see what those things are is how a weaned faith is lived out.

The process of having our faith weaned is letting God move us from being fed to feeding ourselves to eventually feeding others. Sometimes that means sacrificing our desires in our individual story for the people God wants to touch in the big story. God may want to reach someone else through what is happening right now in your story. The pain or circumstances you may be enduring now are part of what will encourage another person when the end is seen.

When we find ourselves sitting in God's silence, we trust that we will eventually hear His answers. We are assured that God is not ignoring us, but is at work doing more than we know to ask. When our faith is weaned, we do not need God's immediate answer to know God is working. We do not need to have a certain prayer answered to know that we've been heard. Our maturity allows us to wait, knowing God is doing something bigger than we imagine. We can hold our questions and, even when we hear silence, not let go of our faith. God may let us sit in darkness, but when we finally emerge with His answers, the gift of what that time produced is evident. The risk God takes by letting you sit in darkness is worth the prize of your grown-up faith.

> When our faith is weaned, we do not need God's immediate answer to know God is working.

REFLECTION

1. Think of a prayer that God has not answered for you the way you wanted. In light of this psalm, what do you think God might be trying to teach you?

2. Looking at your faith and how it's matured, would you say you are at the stage of being fed, feeding yourself, or feeding others? What step could you take to move to the next level of maturity?

3. Have your prayers evolved or changed since you first began following Christ? If so, how?

20

Looking Back for Our Future

PSALM 143:5

I remember the days of long ago; I meditate on all your works and consider what your hands have done.

In order to see our way forward, we sometimes have to look backward. The rearview mirror can provide our best view of God's work. Looking back at what God has done helps you persevere in the midst of what is or is not happening in your life right now. You can trust that the same God who acted then is with you now—even if He is working in ways you may not be able to see. Looking back also reveals the ways God shaped your past circumstances, so you know that what is going on in your current story may one day look very different. By remembering God's faithfulness in the past, you find the vision you need to see your way ahead.

After pouring out his anguish at the beginning of this psalm, David displays his first ray of hope in these seven words: "I remember the days of long ago." David has to take his thoughts away from his current circumstances to find his hope. We don't know if the "long ago" is David's own past or the past of his forefathers, but both are sources for encouragement in what he faces. David could be thinking of his battle with Goliath, and how God equipped him to conquer a giant who greatly exceeded his strength, which would infuse him with courage. David could also be thinking back further—to how God not only delivered his forefathers from slavery, but parted a sea to protect them. This would remind him of the miracles God is able to do, and give him confidence in his current despair. Whatever is on David's mind as he says these words, he sets the example for us to look back to our memories. In God's faithfulness in the past, we find courage and strength when we don't see where God is right now.

> By remembering God's faithfulness in the past, you find the vision you need to see your way ahead.

David's spiritual practice of remembering is not new; it is referenced in earlier places in Scripture, and it is a practice we are invited to continue. If you find a way to record God's faithfulness, you have a place to return to when life feels dark. God repeatedly called the Israelites to remember throughout the Old Testament because it was when they forgot who God was that they lost their bearings. They needed to remember what God was capable of so they wouldn't give up or lose their way. In the earlier books of the Old Testament, the Israelites had a practice of piling stones when God met them in a certain location. When other Israelites saw those stone altars, they would know God had done something in that place. This reminded the community of the generations of God's faithfulness whenever they were in a current struggle.

Though we may not pile stones today, we need ways to remember God's faithfulness. Whether it's through journaling, art, music, or symbols, we need to remember and record all that God does for us. Then, like David, we have a place to go when we are discouraged or afraid.

"I meditate on all your works," David says, and the word *all* brings insight as to how we should remember. Some of God's works are obvious in their goodness, and looking back on them immediately encourages us. Some of God's works are less obvious but still important—and taking some time to think about them with the insight you now have may bring new meaning and hope. There may be something painful in your past you have wanted to forget because God did not do what you prayed for. With a closer look at what God did, you may find a new perspective that can encourage your faith. Time brings new meaning to past circumstances because you see how those circumstances were used—not only in your life, but in the lives of others. You may also observe something from those circumstances that prepared or positioned you for what was ahead.

The word *meditate* describes the way David remembers—and this helps us see this as more than a quick spiritual practice. David spends time pondering the evidence of God's handiwork, and his word choice encourages us to do the same. When we ponder our past, we discover that God sometimes brought healing through difficulty rather than provision. We may see how we acquired strength from what God allowed us to endure, or how God worked through something He brought to us that was different from what we hoped. This inward strengthening is a gift that takes more than a surface look in order to see. By spending time contemplating the less obvious ways God has worked, we can draw from the deeper things God has done.

David moves from meditating on God's works to considering what God's hands have done. This reference to God's hands is both personal and powerful. We can be assured that the detail God used in fashioning the universe into existence is the same detail He uses in fashioning our stories together. Nothing we face is too big for His strength.

After considering the work of God's hands, David stretches out his own hands for deliverance (see v. 6). One can't help but think of the visual of their hands joining together as they face the enemy that threatens David now. God's hands are big enough to create the universe, but they are also small enough to hold us. And David invites us to remember that, whatever enemy we face, we have God's hands holding ours to help us make it through.

REFLECTION

1. Do you have a way to record God's faithfulness in your life? If not, how could you begin?

2. Looking back, what is one thing that has happened to you that you now see differently? Why?

3. Take a moment to consider the work of God's hands. What about God's creation helps you know that nothing you face is too big for Him?

21

Nothing You Can Carry

ECCLESIASTES 5:15

Everyone comes naked from their mother's womb, and as everyone comes, so they depart. They take nothing from their toil that they can carry in their hands.

When King Tut's tomb was excavated in 1923, it captivated the world and illustrated a stark spiritual truth. Most Egyptian tombs had been raided by grave robbers, so until this moment, no one had a full picture of what these tombs held inside. When they opened Tut's tomb, they found him mummified in a gold coffin. But it was the other treasures in the tomb that captured the world's attention and brought Tut international fame. There were baskets of fruit, jars of wine, three chariots, beautiful linen garments, a fan made of ostrich feathers, jars of perfumes and oils, and hundreds of jewels. These treasures were there to equip him for the afterlife. There was just one problem—they were all still

there. The measures the Egyptians took to prepare Tut were nulli-
fied by what the tomb revealed. No matter how much a person has
acquired, nothing goes with him or her when life here is through.

Ecclesiastes 5:15 holds the message that King Tut's tomb starkly
illustrates. Nothing we've earned, bought, collected, or built will
go with us when we die. Most scholars believe Ecclesiastes was
authored by David's rich and wise son Solomon, but he refers to
himself only as "the Teacher." This title sets the tone of advice
we receive throughout the book about faith and life. Naked you
came and naked you will go, the teacher warns those who will
listen. His words prod us to make worthwhile investments that
will matter while we are here.

At some point, we all come to grips with the fact that our stay
on earth is limited. How much time you think about that will likely
contribute to the way you live while you are here. As healthy, successful, or important as you may feel right now, one day you will
be a memory. Whatever you've done to build the memory people
have of you will be all that is left behind when you die. No matter
how much you acquire or save, one day you will leave this earth
without it. King Tut's tomb is a vivid reminder of what not to live
for during the limited time you are here.

You came with nothing, and that will be the way you depart.
Solomon further qualifies the point by saying you will take nothing
with you that you can carry in your hands. No matter how strategic
you are with your money or assets, none of those things will go
with you. Your homes, businesses, and bank accounts will all be
left behind. Even if you designate where your money will go, someone else will make decisions with your investments that you will
not be here to control. The treasures you collect, the awards you
earn, the money you save—none of it will go with you when you
leave. But there is an insight implicit in the opposite of this verse:
The things you can't carry with your hands will be yours to take.

The investment of words and actions in other people's lives
not only will live beyond you, but will always be a part of you.

What you carry with your hands may be stockpiled around you, but only what is in your soul will go with you when you die. What goes with us after death is not what we acquired, but the impact we made. Keeping this truth in front of us helps us invest in the right things while we are here.

The things we carry *without* our hands are the things that stay with us. This inverted truth of Ecclesiastes 5:15 can help us make decisions about what to do with the time we have. One way to see what you view as important is by taking stock of your calendar alongside your bank account. The ways you spend your time and money provide a reality check for the priorities you have in your life. But more importantly, this verse prods us to look at investments we may *not* be making that will live beyond us. These are the things we think about when we have a sudden health scare or accident that threatens to end our life. Solomon invites us to live every day the way we do after we've had this kind of "brush with death" experience. The things that fill our days are suddenly seen in an entirely new light. Our jobs, tasks, and accomplishments pale in comparison to the relationships and priorities we know are most important. However, as soon as the threat of death leaves us, the urgency to fill our closets, cupboards, and bank accounts woos us back. What we need is a picture of King Tut's tomb as a screen saver or symbol to keep as a reminder in front of us. This would inspire us to reorganize our days toward investments that will live beyond us in the time we have left.

> The investment of words and actions in other people's lives not only will live beyond you, but will always be a part of you.

We will leave this world exactly the way we came, and we will take nothing our hands can carry when that time comes. But we will carry in our souls all the investments we made in others while we were here. Let King Tut's tomb be a reminder of what you will leave behind that will have no lasting importance. And let the people around you become the investments you focus on in the time God has you here.

REFLECTION

1. If you were to die tomorrow, what do think others would say about you or the impact you made while you were here?

2. How does knowing that your time on earth is limited impact the importance you place on your finances and accomplishments? Is there anything you want or need to change?

3. What are the things/relationships/words you keep putting off until later because you think you have more time? How does this verse encourage you to stop putting them off?

22

God's Activity

> ### ECCLESIASTES 11:5
>
> *As you do not know the path of the wind, or how the body is formed in a mother's womb, so you cannot understand the work of God, the Maker of all things.*

You may not be conscious of it, but every day you are presented with dozens of miracles. Starting with the breath you take, things are happening around you—and in you—that are beyond your comprehension or control. In the next twenty-four hours, your heart will beat 104,000 times, you will inhale 23,000 times, and your body will lose and reproduce up to 50 trillion cells. In the next minute, 250 babies will be born, 105 people will die, lightning will strike 6,000 times, and the universe will expand by 2,766 miles. If you stopped to consider all that is going on around you that you don't control, you would recognize how much God is doing and how much He controls. Perhaps it would encourage you to let go of things you try to control and put them in God's hands, where this verse invites them to be.

Ecclesiastes 11:5 begins with the reality of our finite understanding. Just as we don't know the path of the wind or how a baby is formed, we have a limited understanding of how God works. When we pray for our desires, we don't see what God sees about the direction or path our prayers need to take. We see the end—and we make assumptions about what we think should happen to get us there. But God sees things that need to happen along the way that we will only understand when we look back. As our faith grows, we leave more room in our prayers for God's direction in what is happening. We can have peace at any given moment that we are where we need to be.

If you've ever watched the wind blow over a period of time, you know the next breeze is not always predictable. Trees can sway in both directions, and the wind can diminish to a light breeze or grow to devastating strength. Only in retrospect do we really see how strong the wind blew or where it was headed. Perhaps that is why Solomon uses the wind to remind us that God can be trusted to chart our course.

We are also challenged to consider the limits of our understanding by observing how a baby develops before a birth. Just four weeks after conception, this tiny life is already a miniscule miracle. The baby has already started to develop a neural tube from which the brain, spinal cord, and backbone will be formed. From that point forward, what happens inside the womb is nothing short of astonishing. Watching a baby form is one of our best windows to see God at work.

With the analogy of the wind we are invited to make room for God's direction, but with the forming of a baby analogy, we are invited to make room for the details of how God works. In each of these images, we see two distinct ways to trust God with things that are ahead. We are to let God direct us on the path in front of us and trust He has a purpose for what happens

to us along the way. The timing and detail of a baby's development reveal that things have to happen at a certain time and
in a certain way for the baby to be ready for birth. A baby's
circulatory system can't develop until the placenta splits off and
forms a food source. The spinal chord can't develop if the neural tube isn't formed first. The timing of these details shows us
that what is happening right now in our lives may be preparing
us for something that is coming. Not only is God forming our
path of direction, He is putting together the details we will need
when we get there.

We may be praying for what God wants for us, but the path
getting there may be different from what we expect. If we are too
set on the path we want, we may lose out on an important detour.
Only God knows what is around our next bend, and Solomon
is inviting us to trust God's direction for how things unfold. We
may question the circumstances happening right now, but we
will discover one day that they happened for a reason. They may
form a character quality we will need or position us to meet a
person we need to meet, and only in retrospect will we see all that
God did. When we trust God for the direction and details of our
lives, we are acknowledging that the intricacies of God's plan
are beyond what we could ask or imagine.
We learn to pray for God to unfold our lives
in ways only He can arrange from what He
knows and sees.

> The intricacies
> of God's plan are
> beyond what we
> could ask or imagine.

The verse ends by proclaiming God as the
Maker of all things. This acknowledgment
not only gives us a filter for our own prayers,
but helps us in our prayers for everyone else.
If we trust that God has the direction and details of our lives in
His hands, we can also believe He has the direction and details of
the lives of the people we care about. And as we watch for God's
activity around us, we let our prayers be edited and shaped by
His work.

REFLECTION

1. Have you ever been angry with God because of the way a circumstance was unfolding in your life? Did looking back give you a new perspective?

2. Think back to a situation you went through. Can you see where God allowed some things that seemed strange at the time but eventually benefited you or led you in the right direction?

3. Is there a current circumstance in your life where you need to acknowledge that God sees the ending? How can that impact the way you live in that circumstance?

23

The Voice behind You

When I was a child, one of my favorite games was Marco Polo. The object of the game was to not get tagged by the person who was "it." That person was blindfolded and could only find you by listening for your voice. When he or she shouted, "Marco," you had to yell back, "Polo," and if it was one of your friends, you would disguise your voice. Another strategy was to hide behind other people to avoid getting caught. As fun as this game was, it is the opposite of what Isaiah means when he describes God as "a voice behind you." God may be out of your immediate sight, but He makes His presence known and invites you to recognize His voice.

The image of "a voice behind you" also gives us a better picture of how God guides us. God doesn't lead by making us His puppets, but by speaking to us from behind. We have freedom in deciding which path to choose, and God's guidance comes as we listen along the way. The voice behind us moves as we move and speaks to us about the turns and choices in front of us. But those turns and choices will ultimately be ours to make.

"Whether you turn to the right or left, your ears will hear a voice," Isaiah proclaims, indicating that whichever way we go, we will hear God's voice. The verse does not say that the voice will always come before our choice is made. If we deliberately decide to go a different way from where God is prompting us, we may hear a voice prodding us to turn around. If we go the way we are prompted but we're scared, we may hear a voice giving us courage as we move ahead. We may get our directions in concert with our choices, but we will usually know if the way we are going is right.

If we make a wrong turn and keep going, we may be prodded by God's voice telling us to recalculate our direction. But we have to listen to that voice in order to get the new instructions for which way to take. Our wrong turns may make our journey more complicated, but we are never too far off for God to lead us back. Our journey will be shaped by the turns we take. Wrong turns cannot be undone, but they are forgiven and worked into our itinerary. God can also use them to encourage others once we turn around and let Him lead. Wrong turns often become our testimony.

God does not usurp our will by taking away our freedom. His voice continues to lead from behind even when we are heading for a disaster and are unwilling to stop. But the volume of God's voice increases and decreases with our willingness to heed what it says. Turning up our receptivity is one of the greatest spiritual habits we can develop if we want to grow in our faith. When God has the freedom to lead us, He can take us to places that, without Him, we would never see.

So how do we learn to listen to the voice behind us? Just before verse 21, Isaiah describes some of the communicators of God's voice as no longer hidden and now seen. Israel's history of not listening to God's voice has pushed these teachers away, but now that the Israelites are ready to hear God's voice, God is bringing them back to guide His people. The plural *teachers* indicates there were multiple sources from which God's voice could be heard. Israel had prophets and priests and leaders, but in our world, God's voice can be heard through mentors, pastors, or friends. Our teachers can also be literary—books, Bible studies, and various Scripture translations have the potential to deliver God's voice. People you trust can help you discern God's voice and help you confirm if what you heard is for you, and they can help give you confidence as you move forward by faith. The more you position yourself to listen and act on God's voice, the more of God's voice you will continue to hear.

> If you want the great adventures God offers you, take a risk to heed the voice behind you.

The words you hear from God may be written, spoken, or internal, and you will learn to recognize when His guidance comes. But you will have to step out in faith in order to heed it. When you hear "This is the way; walk in it," it may not look like a safe or easy path from your vantage point. You may be tempted to ignore the voice and opt for the safety and comfort of a known path instead. But if you want the great adventures God offers you, take a risk to heed the voice behind you. God sees beyond what you can see and will stay right behind you leading the way.

REFLECTION

1. Have you ever sensed God's direction? Did it happen before you started down a path or after you took your first step? What did it feel like?

2. Have you ever felt like you were going in a direction that God didn't want you to go?

3. Is there a decision or path in front of you that you need direction on? How can you position yourself to hear that direction? Do you feel you should step out in faith or wait for more direction?

24

Lighting Your Own Fires

ISAIAH 50:11

All you who light fires and provide yourselves with flaming torches, go, walk in the light of your fires. . . . This is what you shall receive from my hand: You will lie down in torment.

Let's be honest, the initial read on this verse is a bit depressing. It doesn't exactly make you want to post it to your social media outlets to get people excited about their faith. Ironically, it is positioned immediately after one of my favorite verses in the Bible, which says, "Let the one who walks in the dark, who has no light, trust in the name of the Lord" (v. 10). I had never seen the warning that comes after it when I first memorized these encouraging words. The context of these verses together shows that the encouragement to trust cannot be heard without the warning of what happens when we *don't* trust. The imagery of verse 11 keeps us holding on to God when we are tempted to give up the wait and find our own way out.

When you walk in the light of *your* fires, you are not waiting for the light of God's fire. You are deciding you cannot wait any longer for God's guidance, and you are going to guide yourself instead. This verse says that if you do that, you *will* walk in the light of *your* fire. You are deciding not to wait for God's light, and the consequences from that point on will be yours to bear. The warning in this verse is the torment we inflict on ourselves when we don't wait for God and attempt to find our own solutions. This verse is our lifesaving admonition of the misery that solutions apart from God can ultimately bring.

Frankly, striking out on your own can feel a lot better than continuing to sit in the dark. At the very least, when you make a move to find your own solution, you feel you are making strides toward the goal you seek. The problem is, when you move out ahead of God's time (as you may have already discovered), you can make things a lot more complicated. There may be immediate satisfaction, but there is often pain down the road. You may feel you are finished waiting in the dark, but if God still has you there, it is usually for a reason. There may be something happening that you will need once God brings you into the light. If you short-circuit the timing, you may come out of the dark the same way you went into it. You will miss the gifts God wanted to give you—and you may discover you need them as time unfolds.

Hope for the Flowers by Trina Paulus (Paulist Press, 1972) is the story of a friendship between two caterpillars. All the caterpillars around them have joined a pile of climbing caterpillars in a quest to reach the sky. Initially the two of them join the pile, but one gives up because she recognizes the futility. She goes to a tree all by herself, and after a period of time in the darkness, she comes out with her wings. When her caterpillar friend sees her, he sees something that happened to her in her time in the darkness that he also needs. The allegory behind this story is similar to the message of Isaiah 50.10–11. We grow in the darkness, and when we short-circuit or avoid it, we end up missing a part of our development that we need.

Whether your darkness is extended singleness, a painful marriage, an unsatisfying job, or something else, when you attempt to move out of your situation too soon, you may miss out on what God has for you. It's not that you should resolve to spend your life in the darkness, but there may be a season of waiting in the dark that you may need. God works *in* us while we are waiting for God to work things out *around* us. When the end of our wait comes, we are equipped for what awaits us there.

> We grow in the darkness, and when we short-circuit or avoid it, we end up missing a part of our development that we need.

Not only should we wait for what is happening to us in the dark, we also need to trust that things are being prepared around us. If we rush the timing to emerge too soon from the darkness, we may miss out on what will eventually be there. Only in retrospect will we understand the timing of all God has for us when we emerge from the darkness.

What we believe about the dark often paves the way for our decisions in the dark. If we believe nothing is happening, we may be moved to make things happen because we feel God doesn't care. We might feel neglected in our pain or fear and feel that God has abandoned us. But God holds every moment of our darkness in His heart, and these verses assure us He is with us there.

You may feel at times that you cannot wait any longer. In one of my own seasons of darkness, I came close to abandoning the wait and striking out on my own. But choosing to believe God was working in the darkness made the difference in how I lived it, and what God was doing was woven together in perfect timing—which I could have easily imagined was too late. The longing we may feel during our time in the darkness makes the joy that much sweeter when God leads us out of it. That is the mysterious gift Isaiah 50:11 warns us not to miss.

REFLECTION

1. Are there any areas of your life where you are "lighting your own fires"? In light of this verse, what actions can you take to remedy that?

2. Looking back on seasons of darkness in your life, how did God work in you in those seasons? How did He work around you? Did this position you for what happened next?

3. How do you balance moving forward with waiting on God? What helps you discern what you should do?

25

Build Houses and Settle In

JEREMIAH 29:5

Build houses and settle down; plant gardens and eat what they produce.

don't know about you, but when I find myself in a place I don't want to be (emotionally or circumstantially), my temptation is to keep my bags packed. I have my eye on the door, and my prayers are focused on God helping me get out. Yet here in this verse, we find words that encourage us to do exactly the opposite. I find it interesting that in the same chapter that carries such a hopeful promise for our future (see v. 11) there is also strong encouragement to stay in the now. Even if the now is a place we would rather not be.

Exile can be a place you don't want to be, circumstances you'd rather not have, or an unfulfilled longing. The heading at the beginning of this chapter of Jeremiah is "A Letter to the Exiles," and it is addressed to the Israelites after they were taken to a location none of them wanted to be. They had been captured by King Nebuchadnezzar and taken from their homes to Babylon, and we can only imagine how much they longed to return to Israel. Yet Jeremiah's words encouraged them to settle in where they were and stay because there was a purpose for their time in Babylon. During our own seasons of exile, we might be watching the door and planning our escape. But God invites us to turn our attention to what this time has for us right now.

"Build houses and settle down" gives us an indication of longevity. Jeremiah doesn't say, "Rent houses and go month-to-month." He tells the Israelites to settle in. I can imagine there was sadness for the Israelites who hoped their time in Babylon would be brief and temporary. These people would discover that their exile would last seventy years (see v. 10), and it would be a lifetime for some in their midst. Clearly God did not want them to live their entire time in exile just waiting to be rescued out of it. There were things God wanted them to discover and learn about themselves in exile, and it is the same with us. Exiles are not mistakes or placeholders. They are for a purpose that we are invited to take the time to see.

"Settle down" is a phrase a teacher would say to a group of restless children. Perhaps this was encouragement the Israelites needed to hear in the restlessness of being away from the comfort of home. When we are in a place we don't want to be, whether physically, emotionally, or spiritually, it is natural to feel uneasy and restless. This call to settle down feels very incongruous with what our hearts naturally feel. Nevertheless, God tells us we need to slow down in order to see what our circumstances might bring. "Settle down" can also be a helpful prayer when we are occupied with future worries. God is always in the present, and no matter what the present looks like, it is where He wants us to be.

"Plant gardens and eat what they produce" also gives the inkling of longevity. Apparently, the Israelites were going to see houses built and crops rise, and they were encouraged to contribute to the good of where they were. "Plant gardens" has a service element to it and could be interpreted as an encouragement to do what we can for the good of those around us. Even when we are somewhere we would rather not be, God invites us to participate in the lives of the people who are there. In seasons of want and longing, it can feel too hard to connect with others, and we may be tempted to isolate. When we reach out to people, however, a mysterious healing occurs. The pain of our exile dissipates when we get involved in the lives around us. God has designed us for community, and when we reach out to help those around us, our own lives are fulfilled.

Exile may mean letting go of some of the dreams we have for ourselves and letting them be replaced with dreams God has for us. While there is almost always loss in exile, there can also be great joy when we engage in what God has for us there. This is what Jeremiah encourages the Israelites to do. God wants the Israelites to work for the good of the land they are *in*, even though it is not the land where they hoped to be. As we think of the Israelites eating what their gardens produce, we imagine gatherings around the table. These gatherings were probably placeholders of joy in the midst of the season of exile they were called to endure. "Eat what they produce" brings hope that we will have moments of great joy in the midst of our difficulty. When we enjoy those moments and savor what they give our souls, we will find our exile is a less painful sentence to have to endure.

> We may not be able to choose what happens to us, but we can choose our response to what God wants to develop in us.

Whether our exile is a place we don't want to be, a circumstance we would rather not have, or an unfulfilled longing we are called to bear, this verse gives us great wisdom and insight for our seasons of exile. In these seasons, we may not be able to choose what happens to us, but we can choose our response to what God wants to develop in us. This is the gift our exile offers—an

111

opportunity to grow our soul in a way that no other season can bring. The calling of this verse is not just to endure it, but to live it.

REFLECTION

1. Are you someone who lives in the present, or are you often dwelling on what happened yesterday or what may happen tomorrow?

2. How have you lived your exiles? Are you in one now? Can you think of moments of joy you've had during an exile period?

3. How do you feel about settling in to your next season of exile differently? Is there any advice from this verse that resonates with you?

26

The Writing on Our Hearts

> ### JEREMIAH 31:33
>
> *This is the covenant I will make with the house of Israel. . . . I will put my law in their minds and write it on their hearts. I will be their God, and they will be my people.*

There comes a time in parenting when you yearn for your child to "get it." For my husband and me, that time came when our boy turned fourteen. You watch to see if your child starts doing homework without your bugging him, brushes his teeth without being told, and occasionally cleans his room before he goes to school (we settled for once a week). Your hope is that eventually your child will want to do these things because he sees the good in them. But your deepest hope is that the love underneath your commands will one day be seen. That may be a little of what God feels in this verse.

When we reduce our relationship with God to a scale, we are measured by the good and bad we offer Him. In this verse, God overrides that measurement and gives us an unconditional declaration of His love. This promise is to the future house of Israel, which extends beyond the Israelites to include all believers. With the language of resolve, God declares through Jeremiah that a new covenant *will* be made. God *will* put His law in our minds and hearts, He *will* be our God, and we *will* be His people. The word *will* is used four times in this verse, emphasizing the unwavering decision God has made. In this new covenant, our obedience no longer dictates the relationship we have with Him.

From prior verses in Jeremiah, it is clear that God wanted more than obedience to a set of commandments to seal our relationship with Him. When God declares that we are His people, we are left with no way to earn what is already ours. In this new covenant, our standing in God's family is based not on what we do but on the identity that God has given us. Like the last name we give our children, our identity is secured because of who we are. "I will be their God, and they will be my people," God says, and with this promise, God puts His family seal on both ends of the agreement. Our relationship is entirely based on God's decision to extend His unconditional love. With the death and resurrection of Jesus, the earth will eventually see this declaration take human form.

The old covenant had been broken too many times, and God recognized the need for more than our wavering obedience to sustain it. We needed a changed heart and mind, and in this new covenant, that's what God promises us. While the first covenant hinged on God's people keeping the law, this new covenant is fulfilled simply by receiving the grace God offers us. When God says, "I will put my law in their minds and write it on their hearts," we are left with nothing to do but open our hearts to what God has done.

The plan for God to give us the Holy Spirit is forecasted in this hopeful promise. This writing on our hearts is an image of the way

the Holy Spirit leads—speaking both audibly and inwardly words that stir in our hearts. Every time you feel prompted to help, reach out, or remember someone, it is an indication that the Spirit is leading you. When you face a fear or hold on to God in spite of obstacles, there is a good chance the Spirit is empowering your faith. When you are nudged to take a faith-directed turn, the Spirit is likely leading your steps. And when you feel convicted of something you did or can't stop doing, the Spirit may be at work at reclaiming your heart.

The difference in this new covenant is that God puts in us what we need to follow Him. So instead of trying to gain God's approval, we simply receive and respond to how God leads. This understanding needs to be refreshed again and again, because our tendency is to measure what God wants from us. This offer of unconditional love seems too good to be true, and even when we speak of it to others, we find it hard to truly grasp what it means for us. But the truth is, nothing you can ever do will make you loved more than you already are.

Read that again.

When you truly understand how much God loves you, your actions begin to flow from God's Spirit expanding within you, rather than from what you think you need to *do* to earn God's love. Responding to God doesn't earn you points; it draws you into God's dreams, which are greater than you can imagine. You are invited to simply receive what God has already decided by calling you His.

> You are invited to simply receive what God has already decided by calling you His.

Your obedience may flow from your relationship with God, but it does not define it. In the new covenant, God has done everything you need to rest in the standing that is yours. God has declared that He is your God, and when you open your heart to Him, you become one of His people. You are free to live from a place of being loved, and you are empowered by His Spirit to live out His purpose in bringing you here.

REFLECTION

1. Do you truly grasp that you can do nothing to change God's love for you? How could that truth impact your daily walk with God?

2. Are you living in response to what God has done, or are you living in your own strength trying to gain God's approval?

3. How often do you feel the Holy Spirit is prompting you? What form does it come in? Is it always the same form?

27

The God Who Breathes
Life and Hope

EZEKIEL 37:3

He asked me, "Son of man, can these bones live?"
I said, "Sovereign Lord, you alone know."

It catches my eye when God asks a person what is possible. It's as if God wants to know the extent of our faith and how much we believe He is able to do. Here in the midst of a valley full of dead bones, God asks the prophet Ezekiel if he believes something can still happen. Ezekiel stands where all of us stand when all we see is emptiness and loss. But when it comes to the way God works, impossibility is the soil of miracles. And the darker things are around us, the more perfect a setting it becomes for God to shine.

Ezekiel's name means "strengthened by God," and he is a prophet to the Israelites when they are exiled in Babylon. His name perfectly defines the ministry he has been called to do. The Israelites are scattered and weakened, and Ezekiel has given them hope by prophesying a future where they will be gathered and strong (see Ezekiel 36). From their vantage point in Babylon, this seems impossible—and that is the perfect setting for what God is about to reveal to Ezekiel. In a valley of bones, Ezekiel is given a vision of miraculous hope to show the Israelites what God is capable of and wants to do.

When chapter 37 first begins, Ezekiel looks around him and sees that he has been set in the middle of a valley. The vision God shows him occurs not on top of a mountain, but in a place where hopelessness so often takes root. We often refer to being in a valley when we are feeling lost and discouraged. Ezekiel's vision speaks most profoundly to people who are in a place of despair. Our places of despair set the stage for hope.

> Our places of despair set the stage for hope.

You aren't looking for hope when you have no reason to need hope. Most of us would like to skip over the experience of despair, but it is our despair that drives our yearning for hope. Loss and desolation provide the backdrop for the miraculous new chapters God wants to open up for us. The emptiness we see holds a promise of what we are asked to believe God can do. In the valley of despair, we have a chance to experience whether or not our faith is real. When Ezekiel looks around him, all he can see are dry, dead bones. As if that isn't enough, God leads him to walk back and forth *through* the bones, so he can see just how dead they have become (see v. 2). I imagine Ezekiel would have been fine with his initial glimpse, but God wanted to be sure he took in the fullness of loss that was around him. Only after Ezekiel has plumbed the depths of the valley does God pose the question of faith in verse 3 that God asks us all.

You notice that Ezekiel doesn't say yes or no to God's question; instead, he puts the question back on God to answer. But the way Ezekiel phrases his response reveals the great faith he has in God. By calling God Sovereign Lord, Ezekiel acknowledges God's power and control over all circumstances. "You alone know" is a prayer that makes room for the miracles God wants to do. Often we are taught that the only way to pray for miracles is to boldly tell God what we want Him to do for us. While the passion behind these prayers is something to strive for, the question of who is serving whom becomes muddled in the boldness of the ask. When we frame our prayers by acknowledging God's sovereignty, we leave room for how God wants to answer them. We understand that God's vision is bigger than ours and that His plan involves much more than we can see. This knowledge shouldn't subdue our prayers but strengthen them—for we pray for God to work and move according to His glory. God often wants to do something much bigger than the prayers we pray.

Ezekiel's response gives us language to use when we feel stuck in a valley. Whether it is a dark time in our own life or the lives of those we care about, shouting out "You alone know!" is sometimes all we can pray. This response can be the doorway to God's miracle unfolding before us. What God is going to do may be something we have never experienced or seen. Certainly that was true for Ezekiel and what he experienced in the verses that follow. When he said, "Sovereign Lord, you alone know," it made room for God to answer in a way he never could have thought to pray. Ezekiel opened his heart to receive the unfathomable miracle God wanted to do.

Ezekiel's openness to God leads to the vision of what is going to happen to the people of Israel. Their nation is dead and gone, and the people are scattered in Babylon with no idea when—or if—they'll ever be home. In front of Ezekiel's eyes, God shows what He will do with Israel by standing up the bones and putting skin on them. God breathes life into the whole valley of bones, and they become an army of people alive, ready to make their way back home.

This vision strengthens Ezekiel's word of hope that he is being called to communicate to the Israelites in Babylon. But this passage reaches beyond the context of Israel to breathe life into the despairing chapters we live too. In this story from Ezekiel, we see a foreshadowing of the resurrection. God reveals not only what He plans to do for the Israelites, but what His plans are for us after we die. The power we witness in Ezekiel's vision is the power God extends to us through Jesus's death and resurrection. When our stories seem over and we feel dead and dry, God promises a second chapter of life.

REFLECTION

1. Think about a time of despair in your life. Did you see any possibility of hope? Why or why not?

2. Do your prayers acknowledge God's sovereignty and ability to answer any way He chooses, or are your prayers mainly a list of specific requests?

3. How could taking on Ezekiel's "Sovereign Lord, you alone know" attitude of prayer change your experience with God?

28

Running Away from God

JONAH 1:5

All the sailors were afraid and each cried out to his own god. . . . But Jonah had gone below deck, where he lay down and fell into a deep sleep.

So much could be said about the book of Jonah, not the least of which is its problem of believability. But without delving into the scientific possibilities of whales swallowing people, what the book of Jonah really communicates is why we need to listen to God's voice. It also conveys rather dramatically what can happen when we don't. An insight I discovered recently is that the name Jonah means "dove." While this book is primarily about a man running away from God, it is also about the way that God pursues him, and the connection of the Holy Spirit to Jonah's name seems like a coincidence we shouldn't miss. The consistent theme throughout this book is that God doesn't let go of Jonah. Through the Holy Spirit we experience the same truth: God doesn't let go of us. Our response to God's Spirit, however, makes the difference in how our story is lived.

When Jonah hears where God wants him to go, he responds by taking off in the other direction. From this point on, Jonah is confronted with God's presence calling him back to his task. When Jonah gets on a boat heading in the opposite direction from where he's supposed to go, the Lord sends a storm to stop him. The storm is so horrendous that the sailors cry out to their gods while Jonah takes a nap. This is where we will pause—and consider how the concept of taking a nap speaks to our faith.

A nap takes many forms in our spiritual journey. Maybe we don't actually go to sleep, but we do other things that lower the volume of God's voice. We may try to escape God's voice by pursuing forms of distraction. The busier we make ourselves, the less space we leave for God to be heard. But like the sound of a running stream or waves in an ocean, God's voice is softly consistent. And occasionally it grows to a volume that rises above our distractions and demands to be heard. In some ways it is comical to picture Jonah catching some Z's while the storm grows violent. If you've ever been on a ship in normal weather, you know it's hard to sleep even when the waves only slightly pick up. But this nap is symbolic of Jonah's response to the mission God has given him. When all else fails, close your eyes and hope the voice will go away. (This behavior is strangely familiar in our teenage son.) But God's voice takes many different forms and has the power to jolt us out of our stupor. And sometimes God even uses the words and actions of people around us to redirect us on our path.

The sailors call out to their gods before Jonah does. Even in their pagan religion, they inadvertently show Jonah up by calling out for help from above. I wonder how Jonah felt when he saw the sailors more conscious of their need for God than he was. Sometimes when we are running away from God, God uses people around us to convict us without even knowing they are a part of God's ploy.

Ultimately Jonah claims responsibility for what is happening—but only after the lots are cast and Jonah is called out. We are left wondering if Jonah would have ever let the sailors know the calamity was his responsibility if they had left him sleeping. He seems to be responding to the circumstances around him rather than ready to listen to what God says. Jonah's progression of unresponsiveness illustrates what happens when we choose not to act on what God is telling us. The more we ignore God's voice, the less we are apt to hear or respond. But the good news of this story is that God goes to dramatic extremes to pursue this unresponsive prophet. Jonah's story becomes an illustration of the grace God offers each of us. God keeps pursuing Jonah, even with all Jonah's efforts to elude Him. And in this extension of undeserved grace, we find great hope.

Ultimately, this verse stirs us to consider why we listen or don't listen to what God is telling us. Jonah was reluctant because God asked him to do something he did not want to do. Extending God's grace to an enemy seemed unthinkable to Jonah, and this prods us to consider what limits we place on God for what He might ask us. When we say, "I'll do anything but _____," we need to consider what that is and if that might be exactly what God wants us to do. Most of us find it's easier to listen to God when we hear something we want to hear from Him. It is when we hear what we *don't* want to hear that our faith is tested and we are suddenly tempted to grow deaf. There are times when God's spirit crashes through our comfort zone to lead us to a place we never thought we'd find ourselves. The question Jonah prompts us to ask is whether we will let God take us there.

> It is when we hear what we don't want to hear that our faith is tested and we are suddenly tempted to grow deaf.

Perhaps Jonah's name means "dove" because his life illustrates the way the Spirit of God pursues us. Jonah's story doesn't speak only about the ways we avoid listening to God's Spirit; it speaks about how God's Spirit chases us and never gives up. No matter how far we run or how many "naps" we try to take, God's voice never stops trying to reach us. But we need to wake up and listen to allow God to move us where He wants us to be.

REFLECTION

1. Has God been asking you to do something that you are avoiding? Why are you avoiding it?

2. Has there been a time when you did not listen to God's voice? If so, what happened?

3. Fill in the blank: "God, I will do anything for you but _____." What is in that blank, and why do you feel that way?

29

The Small Step God Can Use

JONAH 3:4

Jonah began by going a day's journey into the city, proclaiming, "Forty more days and Ninevah will be overthrown."

It may have been the shortest (and least enthusiastic) sermon ever preached. The eight words proclaimed in this verse represent the first step of obedience Jonah was finally willing to take. It's important to note that this step of obedience only came after the grace-filled words "The word of the Lord came to Jonah a second time" (see v. 1). God's grace precedes Jonah's actions, and in this phrase at the beginning of this chapter, we find room for the second chances we need.

It's been a long (and messy) journey getting to this point, but after three days praying and thinking in the belly of the big fish, Jonah has finally come to the conclusion that he will do what God wants him to do. God could have said, "I've found someone else because you couldn't get it together." But God persevered with Jonah and gave him a second chance at this calling. Ninevah was so big that it required three days to visit; more than 120,000 people lived there (see 4:11). One prophet reaching that number of people seems impossible, but that may be part of why God called Jonah to do it. Jonah was merely to be the mouthpiece; how the Ninevites responded would be up to God. This encourages us to remember that the way God's word is heard is always beyond our power and control.

Perhaps there is a word here for when we hold ourselves back from sharing the gospel because we are afraid of what people will think of us. We get caught up in how people will respond, which is the part we can't control. Our willingness to step out and speak is the only thing God needs from us to do His work. The message Jonah delivered to the Ninevites was stark, and he did nothing to embellish it. Yet the response of the Ninevites outweighed anything Jonah could have said. Clearly, the power behind Jonah's words was way beyond Jonah. Somehow, the words were enough for God to powerfully use them, and the scope of the response of the Ninevites bears this truth.

Jonah's obedience is a bit like that of a child who is asked to apologize when he is not really feeling it. The tone you hear may not be exactly what you have in mind, but you accept it because the child has done what you asked. Obedience is not always about having the perfect words or intention. It's stepping out with a willingness to do what God says in spite of how you may feel. Perhaps that is an encouragement to all of us that we don't have to wait until we are completely ready or our motivation is right to serve God. Instead, we can offer up our fear, unwillingness, and doubt and let God use what we have. "Jonah obedience" allows us to experience the grace-filled power that infuses even our smallest step.

God's call to Jonah stayed exactly the same, but what changed was how Jonah responded to it. The difference between chapter 1 and chapter 3 reveals the weight of our response in how our story unfolds. God has orchestrated the world in such a way that our response to

God makes a difference in what happens in our story. Though God is sovereign in His ultimate plans, this account of Jonah confirms that we are not controlled like puppets. We play a significant part in how our story unfolds. God's quest with Jonah illustrates that God will go to great lengths to fulfill His calling for us. But our response to God is what helps write the story of how this calling takes shape.

Though Jonah did not want Ninevah to receive God's grace, he had to be amazed at the turn these people were willing to make. The next verse describes how the Ninevites immediately declared a fast, and spread the news all the way to the king. When the king heard Jonah's words, he covered himself with sackcloth and extended the fast to include even the animals. The response to Jonah's call so far outweighed the call itself that it left no doubt about God's power. Maybe in using Jonah, God intended to reveal just that.

> The promise of a second chance is ours when we are ready to say yes to what God asks.

Scholars may struggle with whether Jonah's story actually happened, but it is the one Jesus chooses to reference when He is asked for a sign to prove who He is (see Matthew 12:38–40). The fact that Jesus aligns himself with this story reveals an importance to Jonah's ministry that extends beyond Ninevah. Not only do we see a foreshadowing of Jesus's death and resurrection in this story, but we witness the extension of God's grace to people who seem out of His reach. The boundaries of God's love are stretched to touch those we would judge unworthy of it. And Jonah teaches us that the promise of a second chance is ours when we are ready to say yes to what God asks.

REFLECTION

1. Are there people you feel are beyond God's grace or don't deserve it? Why?

2. What, if anything, holds you back from telling others about God's gift of grace? Where does this obstacle come from—your confidence in yourself, your belief in God, or something else?

3. Do you feel you need to have all the answers before you step out to be an ambassador for the faith? Why or why not? How does Jonah's story encourage you?

30

Defiant Faith

HABAKKUK 3:17-18

Though the fig tree does not bud and there are no grapes on the vines, though the olive crop fails and the fields produce no food, though there are no sheep in the pen and no cattle in the stalls, yet I will rejoice in the Lord, I will be joyful in God my Savior.

In the late 1800s, Horatio Spafford was about to leave on a needed vacation. His family had been through incredible difficulty, and he felt it was time to take them away. At the last minute, Horatio was detained by some work, so he sent his wife and four daughters on a ship ahead of him. Just before his own boat was to depart, he received the devastating news that their ship had been in an accident, and all four of his daughters had drowned. Because his wife was found unconscious, Horatio boarded his boat so he could accompany her home. As his ship passed over the place where the tragedy occurred, Spafford wrote words that have encouraged millions of people in their darkest times. "It Is Well with My Soul" penetrates your soul and woos your tattered faith back to life.

I've always wondered if Habakkuk was an inspiration for Spafford to write this hymn in the midst of his tragedy. Certainly, the common themes between their songs have caused others (besides me) to take note. The short book of Habakkuk is a manifesto of faith, calling us to hold on to God when circumstances rail against us. Habakkuk gives us language for when we are grasping for our trust.

Habakkuk wrote few words, but they are a tribute to a faith that was tested. He served during a confusing time in Israel's history, when God was allowing evil nations to conquer them in order to provoke their faith. Habakkuk is perplexed by what he sees, and when he cries out to God for explanation, God never answers him. Instead, by widening Habakkuk's perspective, God shows him that He is in control. Here we see a theme we notice throughout Scripture—that sometimes we need to look at the bigger story to see that God is working. God rarely explains His actions; instead, He shows us that there is always more going on than we can see. This is what Job 42, Psalm 73, and Habakkuk 3 all communicate. What our circumstances present to us is not the full picture of what will eventually be revealed.

So how can these words from Habakkuk encourage us today when our lives are so different from his? Consider the meaning behind the imagery Habakkuk uses to reaffirm his faith. "Though the fig tree does not bud and there are no grapes on the vines" speaks to when we cannot see what God is doing. These descriptions hold hope and promise because the fruition of what will happen is not yet visible to our eyes. The time *before* the figs and grapes appear, however, is important—for without this time of nourishment and watering, those fruits cannot grow. Habakkuk is encouraging us to remember that this time is necessary for what will ultimately appear.

As Habakkuk moves on in his song, his trust grows more defiant. You can almost see his faith grow stronger with each phrase. "Though the olive crop fails and the fields produce no food" is a cry of loss rather than of promise. Here he is saying that even when it appears that God did not come through, Habakkuk is holding on—believing that one day he will have a different perspective on what he currently sees. Perhaps our loss is making room for new hope, or our need is making room for the way God will meet it. Habakkuk is saying he will hold on in spite of loss and heartbreak, believing God's deliverance will come. Like Horatio Spafford, he is proclaiming that the despairing circumstances around him will not dictate the condition of his soul.

"Though there are no sheep in the pen and no cattle in the stalls" is an indication of emptiness. Different from the loss represented in the previous phrase, this symbolizes Habakkuk's void. The words speak to holding on to God's timing for His provision and having the willingness to wait in the emptiness. His words challenge the "health and wealth" gospel that says abundance is the only indication of God's blessing on your life. In a sense, Habakkuk is saying, "Neither wealth nor need define God's blessing, and this season of emptiness and want will not define God's love for me. I will hold on whether God gives me what I want or not." Whether in plenty or in want, Habakkuk encourages us to stand firm in our faith.

Perhaps there is also a word in these verses about proclaiming our faith in the middle of the story. Habakkuk shows us that before God comes through, we have an opportunity to declare our trust. Often, we wait until the end of the story before we share our hope—when the need has been fulfilled and the bow is tied. We need more testimonies from people like Habakkuk, who declare their hope in the middle of their need. When things are going great, people aren't as interested in hearing our story. But when we are clinging to God in spite of nothing we've been given, people draw in and take note. The middle of the story is the time to let our faith shine.

Habakkuk ends with a declaration of his trust. But it is not grim resolve—it is a proclamation of joy. To end this way seems puzzling when we consider the circumstances that brought him to this point. "Lord, nothing good is happening, I see loss and devastation, I am empty and in need . . . yet I will rejoice." If Habakkuk had used *and* instead of *yet*, this verse might feel fake or seem like an expression of inappropriate emotions in tragedy. The *yet* makes this verse a defiant cry of an unwavering faith. We are led by Habakkuk into a prayer that says, "I will rejoice—not because of what is happening in my circumstances, but in the face of them." This is the Spafford-Habakkuk faith we are invited to, the faith which, in the end, God loves to see.

> The middle of the story is the time to let our faith shine.

REFLECTION

1. Have you ever witnessed anyone declaring their faith in God in the midst of tragic or terrible circumstances?

2. When you face difficulty, are you able to lift your eyes to consider the bigger story God is writing? Why or why not?

3. Looking back, where could you have given a testimony in the middle of your story? How might you be able to do that now?

31

Goodness Is Not Forgotten

MATTHEW 1:6

David was the father of Solomon, whose mother had been Uriah's wife.

t's easy to miss if you aren't looking for it. Nestled within Jesus's family tree, we see mentioned a man who was not a part of His line. It is especially noticeable because this particular genealogy (as opposed to the one in Luke 1) follows the line of Joseph, so all the other men mentioned played a part in carrying Jesus's family seed. In the orchestration of this small detail, God made sure that this great man would not be missed.

Uriah is remembered in the Old Testament as a small sidebar in David's story with Bathsheba (see 2 Samuel 11). He is the discarded victim of David's bad choice. But here in Matthew 1, Uriah is brought back and placed before us. Among the women mentioned from Jesus's line, Bathsheba is recorded as "Uriah's wife." This seems too deliberate to be an accident, since Bathsheba is only in there because of her marriage to David. Their son Solomon fulfilled the prophecy about the Messiah coming from David's house. Bathsheba was the wife God chose to bring forth the seed that would connect David to Jesus. Yet she is remembered for all time as Uriah's wife.

Each of the women named in Jesus's genealogy represent God's grace woven into the coming of Jesus. One birthed her son through desperate deception (Tamar); another was a prostitute (Rahab); the third was a widow grafted in from a foreign land (Ruth). Bathsheba's story, however, is perhaps the most grace-filled, because she was stolen by David from her husband. David had many wives who could have carried his seed into the genealogy of Jesus, but God chose Bathsheba, which seems a curious choice. Perhaps this is a window into the messiness behind God's grace. It is also a testimony that goodness is not forgotten. Uriah's life is remembered and honored in this small but significant verse.

The fact that Uriah was a Hittite makes his story of faithfulness to God even more poignant. His devotion to God surpassed David's when he refused to bed his wife while Israel was at war. At each turn of David's planned cover-up, Uriah refused to submit to David's suggestion. Uriah's dedication ultimately cost him his life because he would not budge his single-minded allegiance during his service to God. Uriah unintentionally became God's instrument to bring David to the truth of what he had done.

The prophet Nathan came to bring David's hidden sin to light by telling a story that was symbolic of what he had done. It was about a shepherd whose only lamb was stolen (see 2 Samuel 12), and when David shouted out to condemn the thief, he inadvertently condemned himself. David honored Uriah's life by crying out on Uriah's behalf—even though he himself was the perpetrator of the crime. Although David was forgiven by God, his life would never completely shake this terrible tragedy. The betrayal he endured in his own life from one of his sons filled his life with difficulty and remorse; but from the point of his adultery on, David's devotion to God remained steadfast and unbroken. Psalm 51 reveals that after Nathan's confrontation, David became a witness to God's grace and new starts.

Imagine if the story had been different, and instead of Uriah resisting David's urge, he agreed to go home and sleep with Bathsheba. They might have gone on to have this child fathered by David, with Uriah possibly still in the dark. Uriah's marriage would have been marked by shame and tragedy, resulting in a sorrow Uriah would have had to bear the rest of his life. Ultimately, Uriah was spared this embarrassment by dying with honor. He never had to live with the terrible knowledge that his wife had been impregnated by the God-fearing leader he served.

From this angle, we see a measure of God's grace in how this unfortunate story unfolded. David was left to bear the shame of what he did, and he would carry the sadness of this betrayal to his grave. Uriah not only is remembered as a devoted soldier, but holds a unique place in Jesus's genealogy as a God-honoring Hittite. His presence there, with other non-Israelites, may be a foreshadowing of God's plan to reach all people through His Son.

Matthew 1 reveals that God's story is shaped in part by our small stories and is being woven through our individual lives and choices. With the names leading up to the birth of Jesus, we are reminded how brief our earthly lives are— and why we are here. What is remembered after we are gone is the part we had in God's story

> What is ultimately remembered is the part we had in God's story and the way we played our part.

and the way we played our part. Uriah's brief life granted him little time, and no children to carry on his seed. Yet he is included by name in the genealogy of the Messiah, and he is the only man outside of Jesus's line to have a part. Furthermore, Uriah's devotion to his wife and God are celebrated in how he is listed. The mother of Solomon who passed on the seed to Jesus would always be remembered as Uriah's wife.

REFLECTION

1. Does this new take on Uriah and his story cause you to look differently at a situation you are currently in or have been in in the past? If so, how?

2. Has there been anything unfair in your life or in the life of someone you know that you now see in a new light?

3. In what way(s) do you need to see goodness not being forgotten in your life?

32

When Circumstances
Bring Doubt

MATTHEW 11:2-3

When John, who was in prison, heard about the deeds of the Messiah, he sent his disciples to ask him, "Are you the one who is to come, or should we expect someone else?"

He was born to prepare the way for the Messiah, but in this verse, he seems plagued by doubts. Something has caused John the Baptist to question the mission he came to fulfill. As he sits in jail, he suddenly feels compelled to ask Jesus if He is the Messiah. It seems too late for this question, especially when you consider all that John has said and done up to this point. From the womb on, John seemed certain of Jesus's identity; Luke 1:41 records that he leaped inside Elizabeth's womb when Mary entered the room. But John's circumstances have discouraged him enough to question whether Jesus was actually the one he was born to precede. In this scene from John the Baptist's life, we learn that God makes room for our doubts.

Jesus's trajectory has somehow caused John to rethink his certainty that Jesus is the Messiah, and the confident words he declared in Matthew 3:14 and John 1:29 have been called into question by the behavior he sees in Jesus now. It is starting to become clear that Jesus's kingdom is different from what John thought it would be. John's feelings are not unlike ours when we witness the suffering and godlessness in our world and wonder why God is not intervening. What we learn from John the Baptist is that we can approach God with these questions—and let God know our doubts have rattled our belief.

John boldly sends his messenger to Jesus, and he doesn't do much to hide the confusion embedded in his question. What is important is how Jesus answers—and what His response means not only for John the Baptist but for us. "Report to John . . . the blind receive sight, the lame walk," Jesus begins (see vv. 4–5), and we imagine John wants to hear, "and the prisoners are released." But Jesus doesn't include that phrase in His answer, and John discovers in the fact that he *isn't* released that God's plan encompasses more than his earthly life. The kingdom God is building is eternal, and Jesus is a different Messiah from the political leader John had imagined. In order for John to observe God's kingdom unfolding, Jesus calls him to look beyond his immediate circumstances to see God at work.

It's interesting to note that after Jesus answers John's question, He points to John himself as evidence that His kingdom is different. People in that time expected a different kind of prophet to announce Jesus's arrival than a man feasting on wild honey and bugs. But Jesus points out that this is another sign of God's kingdom being different from what people expected. Neither John nor Jesus acted or appeared the way people thought they should, and they are evidence that God's kingdom is different—and bigger than we can see.

Our circumstances can look grim, so in order to affirm that God is still at work, we may have to lift our eyes to strengthen our faith. John is huddled in a jail cell, unable to continue his ministry, and his circumstances have clouded his judgment. I imagine he is thinking that if Jesus really is the Messiah, this would not have happened, or at the very least, Jesus would get him out. John sees nothing around him that supports his faith, and now he wonders if it's all been a delusion. Jesus's actions have betrayed the faith John had in Him, and John will need a different—and bigger—faith in order to proceed. When Jesus sends back the answer that people are being healed and ministry is happening, John has to look past his own circumstances in order to see it. This will take a spiritual maturity to trust Jesus in what He is doing, even if it isn't what John wants it to be.

Like John, we may not see things resolved the way we want them to be, and we may need to let go of who we think God should be. But Jesus makes it clear that there are places to witness God's glory if we are willing to look beyond our circumstances. The story God is weaving together often differs from what our immediate vision allows us to see.

Jesus ends His response to John's messengers with words that appear to foreshadow the difficulty John will endure at the end of his life: "God blesses those who do not fall away because of me" (v. 6 NLT), Jesus says, and they are words John will have a chance to live. John's life will end gruesomely because he speaks out against King Herod's corruption all the way to his death. Given John's courage moving forward to his death, it is possible his faith may have been strengthened by Jesus's answers to the doubts he had. But one thing we know through verse 11 is that Jesus makes it clear that John's questioning has not rattled Him. He expresses His admiration for John by saying that no one on earth is greater—and affirms

> When we move away from God in our doubts, we sometimes end up abandoning Him. God invites us to move *toward* Him with our doubts instead.

John for being exactly who he is supposed to be. It appears that John's question to Jesus, however offensive it might look to us, was met with Jesus's affirmation. Our doubts don't shake the love God holds for us.

When we move away from God in our doubts, we sometimes end up abandoning Him. God invites us to move *toward* Him with our doubts instead. John's bold question to Jesus gives us courage to ask our own questions and give God a chance to answer them. This opens the door for God to reveal himself in a new way, which can reconstruct our perceptions and strengthen our faith.

REFLECTION

1. Have you ever discussed your doubts about God with anyone or prayed about them? What happened?

2. What does this reflection cause you to realize about your faith? Are you encouraged or discouraged by this account of John the Baptist? Why?

3. What events in your life—or in the world—have caused you to doubt God? What did these events do to your faith?

33

The Answer You Weren't Looking For

MARK 2:5

When Jesus saw their faith, he said to the paralyzed man, "Son, your sins are forgiven."

It must have been at least a little embarrassing to be there in that room and witness this awkward moment. Forgiveness of sins was obviously not what the four friends were looking for when they lowered their paralyzed friend at Jesus's feet. As they dug through the roof, I imagine the packed room grew silent as people held their breath for what would happen next. When they heard the words Jesus finally spoke, the four men who held their friend had to have been disappointed. In the unfolding of this story, we learn God's priority for the things we pray.

When the roof crashed down, all eyes must have been on Jesus to see how He would handle the interruption. The first words out of His mouth would be given more attention than anything else He said. Imagine the shock that rippled through the room when He proclaimed, "Your sins are forgiven." The religious leaders were undoubtedly mortified, the rest of the audience perplexed, but the four friends had to be taken off guard, because Jesus's response was so different from what they had obviously planned. Their experience is not unlike how we feel when we ask for a healing and that prayer is not answered the way we wanted. We have to trust that God sometimes answers us with something even more important than we know to pray.

Eventually Jesus miraculously healed the paralyzed man's body. The people were amazed—but subsequent passages show that was not what they remembered most about this scene. Jesus hijacked the healing by forgiving the man's sins, and the authority He displayed convinced the religious leaders that He was dangerous. He was exercising a power that belonged to God—and now they felt He had to be stopped. Others who were there saw that Jesus was more than a miraculous healer. The authority He commanded with His forgiveness, though less visible than the physical healing, revealed more about who Jesus was claiming to be. From this point forward, Jesus would not be able to be seen as just a healer or a teacher, and His ministry would be marked with horror and belief.

This verse also reveals that Jesus observed the faith of the paralytic's friends before He spoke words of forgiveness that from here on out would set Him apart. Maybe Jesus knew the friends' initial disappointment would become an opportunity to grow a deeper faith. By their bold determination to crash through a roof, these friends showed a confidence in Jesus that was big enough to allow their faith to be stretched. Ultimately, their friend got the healing they came for, but it was the healing they didn't come for that changed their faith.

God's agenda is always moving our faith further and deeper. Just when we think we've got God down, something happens that either explodes or expands our faith. The crowd left this event divided because of what Jesus claimed by offering forgiveness. They all recognized His proclamation of deity, and their different responses revealed which way their faith went. Jesus was intentional in what He wanted to accomplish by the way He orchestrated this healing. He purposely pushed the envelope, so no one would be confused about who He was claiming to be. Perhaps there is a word in this story for people who may affirm Jesus as a healer or teacher but can't affirm His deity. The events of this healing reveal that Jesus doesn't let us partition our belief.

> Just when we think we've got God down, something happens that either explodes or expands our faith.

As C. S. Lewis points out in *Mere Christianity*,

> A man who was merely a man and said the sort of things Jesus said would not be a great moral teacher. He would either be a lunatic—on a level with the man who says he is a poached egg—or else he would be the Devil of Hell. You must make your choice. Either this man was, and is, the Son of God; or else a madman or something worse. You can shut Him up for a fool, you can spit at Him and kill Him as a demon; or you can fall at His feet and call Him Lord and God.*

This challenge, which Lewis so eloquently presents, is what the crowd was forced to confront.

When the paralyzed man was initially lowered, everyone focused on what they obviously saw about this man's condition. But it was what the crowd couldn't see that Jesus focused on first. In the order of His responses, Jesus showed that the healing of this man's soul was infinitely more important than the healing of his body. Though invisible to the human eye, this was the only part of him that would last beyond this life. In this weighty moment, we see that what is invisible to us is what God values most when He looks at us. And in this passage Jesus reveals that the healing

*C. S. Lewis, *Mere Christianity* (New York: HarperCollins, 2001), 53.

we need could be something we might not ask for or never would have guessed.

REFLECTION

1. Think about the prayers that God has not answered the way you hoped. What effect did they have on your faith? Can you see now how God may have been answering a different need for you?

2. Have you ever considered that your faith could inspire God to act? How does that make you feel?

3. Are there any characteristics or attributes of God that you have trouble believing? What are they, and why?

34

When You Have Turned Back

LUKE 22:32

*But I have prayed for you, Simon, that your faith
may not fail. And when you have turned back,
strengthen your brothers.*

He knows when Jesus calls him by his birth name, something is different. Jesus had named him Peter "the rock," but by calling him Simon, Jesus indicates that it is the non-rock part of him He wants to address. Jesus knows Peter is about to fall, and He wants Peter to know He'll be there to hold him. And at the end of the verse, Jesus imparts a mission for Peter to do after he comes through.

Whether we have blown it once, twice, or a thousand times, we see a picture here of God's infinite grace. But we also learn from this verse that Jesus prays for us in our battles and proclaims that, even if we fall, God will see us through. So often we think temptation ends with either victory or failure, but Jesus suggests that the story continues. What happens after we fall is as important as the battle itself, and it can determine our continued course of faith. At the beginning of verse 31, Jesus repeats Simon's name twice. He wants to be sure Peter takes in what He is about to say. By addressing him as Simon, Jesus is reminding Peter that he has another identity besides "the rock" still within him. Peter's humanity is where Satan will strike, and because he feels like a superhuman Jesus follower at this point, it is Peter's pride that Satan will tempt. Peter's confidence will eventually be a powerful tool God will use to unleash His kingdom. But every strength has its weakness, and it is the vulnerable side of Peter's confidence that Satan will attack.

Jesus has just told Peter that Satan has asked to "sift him." This insight about temptation is similar to what we saw in Job. God does not cause our trials, but this verse clearly indicates that God allows them. God uses our trials and temptations for what they will produce in our faith. In the big picture, Peter's confidence needs to be sifted to bring forth more of his humility. His denial of Jesus will help him have compassion and understanding as he spreads God's kingdom to others who need grace. The experience of needing grace yourself gives you a much better bridge to impart grace to others. Peter will eventually become a dispenser of what he needs to receive.

It is interesting to note in this verse that Jesus doesn't pray that Peter will not fall; He prays instead that Peter's *faith* will not fall. This small detail makes room for the fact that Jesus knows what is going to happen next. After a failure, we have a choice—and Jesus is praying for that choice for Peter. We can define ourselves by failure and give up, or do what Jesus tells Peter to do and turn back. Jesus's prayer is that Peter's failure will not keep him from the grace available to get back on his road of faith.

Jesus gives another gift to Peter in this verse by saying, "*When* you turn back," not "*If* you turn back." This confidence from Jesus is something Peter will need when he is wondering whether he has the strength to do what repentance requires. The Peter who says to

Jesus, "I am ready to go with you to prison and to death" (v. 33), will become the Peter who can't admit to a servant girl that he even knows Jesus. But that weakened, humbled Peter is the one Jesus loves. Jesus proclaims His confidence in Peter because He sees beyond Peter's failure to the heart he has within him. He believes Peter will eventually let his faith rather than his failure define him, and that is all Jesus needs to do the work of grace.

This work of grace is what will grow to define Peter's ministry. After Jesus's death and resurrection, Peter will become a spokesman of this grace, and he will invite every tribe and nation to partake (see Acts 10:34–35). But Peter has to experience his own need for grace before he can effectively pass it on to others. He learns in this verse that his relationship with Jesus is anchored not by his success or failure, but by undeserved forgiveness that is simply his to take.

The last part of this verse is Peter's call to ministry even in the midst of a proclamation of Peter's biggest failure. This reveals that our most effective ministry may actually be born more from our weakness than our strength. Our weakness equips us to come alongside others with a knowledge that only experience will allow. The very thing you may be most embarrassed about could be the very thing God uses to define your ministry. In your willingness to offer it to God, you will find God uses it to minister to others who struggle too.

> The only thing that separates us from God's forgiveness is our own unwillingness to turn back.

At the end of this verse, Jesus says, "When you have turned back, strengthen your brothers." In Peter's call to repentance and subsequent ministry, we find a final insight for our faith. Turning back is not a one-time event; our need for God's grace is continual. Even when we feel we are at our strongest, this verse warns us we may be minutes away from a giant fall. But Jesus's words to Peter bring assurance that God's grace not only follows our falls, but even precedes them. Peter will now be able to encourage others to stand firm in that grace. God's grace is available to cover our actions and heal and strengthen us. The only thing that separates us from God's forgiveness is our own unwillingness to turn back.

REFLECTION

1. Has God ever used a trial you have experienced to strengthen your faith? How so?

2. Does knowing that God allows us to go through temptations to grow our faith give you more confidence in the midst of a current trial?

3. Think of a time when you needed grace. Did that soften your heart to offer others grace? How so?

35

The God Who Weeps

f you want to have success memorizing Scripture, this verse is a great place to start. But even in its brevity, it may communicate more about God's heart than any other verse. "Jesus wept" is found in the middle of the story of the death of Lazarus. Even though Jesus knew He would raise Lazarus from the dead, the unbridled grief of Lazarus's family moved Jesus to tears. In one small verse we see the complex union of God's love and sovereignty. Jesus was partly responsible for the tragedy because it was His purposeful hesitation that allowed Lazarus to die. Yet even knowing the miracle that was ahead, Jesus still grieved with the family. The complexity of God's nature was displayed as He wept for what His actions allowed.

The chapter begins with a planned public demonstration of Jesus's resurrection power. This would be the most dramatic revelation thus far of His authority over death. But this miracle would

149

take place in the midst of a private family moment. Jesus would bring unimaginable joy in the middle of a scene of terrible grief. Because Jesus specifically chose someone dear to Him, this public miracle was also going to be very personal. His relationships with Mary, Martha, and Lazarus were three of His closest relationships with anyone on earth. Because of this personal connection, Jesus was touched deeply by the sorrow that preceded the miracle. Through His display of emotions with them, we get a window into what God feels with us.

When Jesus learned that Lazarus was sick and needed Him, He told His disciples that Lazarus's death would reveal His glory (see v. 4). Verse 5 emphasizes His love for Mary, Martha, and Lazarus, yet when these sisters sent word that Lazarus was sick, Jesus stayed where He was. We can look to Jesus's mysterious actions in this passage when we wonder where God is in our sufferings. What looked to be Jesus's apathy was a deliberate withholding for the joy that was to come. The eternal story is the one Jesus always defers to, but He is willing to sit with us in our chapters of suffering. In Jesus's actions, we see that even when God knows joy is coming, He accompanies us in our grief.

> Even when God knows joy is coming, He accompanies us in our grief.

Jesus waited until Lazarus died and then told His disciples it was finally time to go see him. It seemed too late, but that is often the setup for God's finest work. The deader and darker things are, the better the backdrop for the miracle. And this would be the greatest miracle Jesus would do until He resurrected himself. It was on the way to this miracle, however, that Jesus was met with the unrestrained sadness of Lazarus's dear family. They were not only devastated by the loss, but filled with disappointment that Jesus did not show up. Their Lord and dearest friend seemed to have ignored their urgent messages. In the midst of this disillusionment, Jesus arrived to share in their grief. Before Mary collapsed at His feet, she cried out that if He had been there, Lazarus would not have died. Her disappointment grieved Him, and even though He purposely set this stage, it is apparent her tears went deep into His heart. It seems in choosing this particular family for this miracle, He wanted to feel the depth of the sadness of death before He conquered it. Perhaps feeling this sadness lent to His urgency for what He came to do on the cross.

Just before Jesus wept, Scripture records that Jesus was "deeply moved . . . and troubled" (v. 33). Mary's tears prompted Jesus's grief, and even though He knew those tears would turn to joy, it did not stop Him from entering her pain. Lingering in this moment, we see that even though God knows the glory ahead, He accompanies us in the sorrows this life brings us. We have a God who weeps because He knows the separation and death that burden our hearts and steal joy from our lives.

Jesus's tears in this passage moved some people around Him to say, "See how he loved him!" (v. 36). Others questioned why He did not come and heal Lazarus while he was still alive. When Jesus called to the grave, "Lazarus, come out!" I imagine there were some people who looked at each other and agreed by their expressions that Jesus was a madman. I like to imagine their expressions when Lazarus did as he was told.

After this miraculous event, Jesus's life would be marked with followers and haters. Some recognized Him as the Messiah and King, while others were determined to have Him destroyed. But in the smaller story of Lazarus, Mary, and Martha, we are left to wonder what happened after this miracle. Besides having the best story at parties, it must have been difficult for Lazarus to come back from eternity and die twice. But these three friends of Jesus got the opportunity to see their deepest grief transformed to an unseen miracle. And they may have been the only three who had a seed of hope for what could still happen when Jesus was taken to His death on the cross.

This story reveals that our sorrow can often pave the way for God to thrill us. But this small verse assures us that Jesus doesn't bypass the sorrow before His glory is revealed. When you go through pain and disappointment, you have a God who feels those things with you. Even if He sees great joy ahead, He knows you are in the middle of your story and is *with you* where you are. Hold on to Him—and remember that no matter how it looks, anything can happen. As we've discovered in other verses, darkness is God's best backdrop for glory that will ultimately be revealed.

REFLECTION

1. Does the concept of a weeping God change your feelings about where God is in your suffering?

2. Why do you think God grieves with us even when He knows joy is just around the corner? What does that tell you about Him?

3. How does this account of Lazarus change (or affirm) your view of sadness and suffering? Does the big picture of eternity impact the way you feel about your circumstances?

36

Sent with Our Wounds

JOHN 20:21

As the Father has sent me, I am sending you.

Their hopes have been crushed by disappointment because nothing has turned out the way they thought it would. Now fear keeps them behind a locked door—and their only hope at this point is that no one will turn them in. They left everything behind to follow Jesus and spent three years doing ministry by His side. But they have just seen Him crucified and buried, and they have never felt more lost. Rumors have been swirling that the grave is empty, and some have even imagined they've seen Him. But the prospect of an empty tomb has only increased their fear that they will be suspected of grave robbery, and it may be just a matter of time before the religious leaders show up.

Suddenly, Jesus is with them, and new fear holds them speechless. Seeing the terror of their hearts, Jesus shows them His wounds and calms them with words of peace. The disciples are still taking in the miracle of the moment when Jesus commissions them with a brand-new mission. "As the Father has sent me, I am sending you," Jesus says, and from this point forward, they will be the ones to extend God's reach. It sounds like a straightforward call, but picturing the scene, one wonders if Jesus intentionally displayed His wounds before giving them their mission. Commissioning them with His pierced hands, Jesus may be letting them know their wounds will be part of their call. It is often through our sufferings that God gives us our greatest reach.

We know from other resurrection sightings that Jesus didn't have to come into this scene bearing His wounds. Other accounts reveal that He took on alternate appearances, and people recognized Him by the things He said. Mary thought she was talking to a gardener until Jesus spoke her name (see v. 16). The two men traveling to Emmaus thought Jesus was just another friend walking with them until the words He said burned their hearts (see Luke 24:32). Jesus could have chosen another way to appear before His disciples and be recognized by them. But He chooses to come with wounds still on His body and intentionally displays them to His disciples before commissioning them with their new call.

> It is often through our sufferings that God gives us our greatest reach.

Since this scene precedes the one with Thomas, it seems clear Jesus bares His wounds here for another purpose. Perhaps He wants His disciples (and us) to see that ministry happens in letting our wounds accompany us rather than after we've cleaned them up. These clues call us to notice not only what Jesus says but the way He appears when He says it. The disciples are directed to look at His wounds just before they hear their call.

In Jesus's life, death, and resurrection, we see that the way God chooses to reach the world is by power in weakness. When it looked like Jesus was at His lowest point, it was the highest honored position His earthly ministry had. Knowing this, we are not surprised by the call He gives His followers to follow His example. From this point forward in the New Testament, power in weakness becomes the trophy Christ followers proudly display. The disciples leave this scene in the upper room and boldly live and die spreading the word about Jesus. Shame no longer hides them away, because they have seen the eternal power of what Jesus's wounds have done.

We don't want to miss the specific words that are further evidence of our wounds being part of our mission. "As the Father has sent me," Jesus begins, and then He continues with, "I am sending you." The enormity of our mission flowing directly from the mission of Jesus is enough for us to ponder with great reverence. But the words He chose give us further reason to reflect. When He says, "As the Father sent me," Jesus alludes to the fact that He was sent to earth to be wounded. His mission was accomplished by His being broken on our behalf. With this example we can look at our own brokenness and find purpose in our pain by becoming a wounded healer. The pain we bear gives us a specific mission and calling, because we are able to reach people who have experienced that same pain too. When Jesus sent out His disciples, they had to see that brokenness was part of their mission. Knowing the sacrifice each disciple would make causes us to wonder if extending His wounds while commissioning them was Jesus's purposeful intent.

Undoubtedly, the disciples had an upside-down view of power after viewing Jesus's brokenness mixed with resurrection glory. They realized in that moment that the kingdom they thought He would bring was far smaller and more limited than the one He brought. The political and earthly hopes that were crushed by Jesus's death were replaced by new hopes in His unimaginable power. And the fear and embarrassment that hid them away no longer held them captive when they were sent out by their wounded warrior's call.

REFLECTION

1. If you knew your pain had a purpose, would it make you look at it with different eyes?

2. What wounds or weakness do you have that God could use? Are you willing to be used in this way? Why or why not?

3. How do you feel about knowing your mission on earth is aligned, in some ways, with Jesus's mission on earth? In what ways are they alike? How are they different?

37

The Power of Our Thorns

> ### 2 CORINTHIANS 12:8-9
>
> *Three times I pleaded with the Lord to take it away from me. But he said to me, "My grace is sufficient for you, for my power is made perfect in weakness."*

When Paul asked God three times for a thorn to be removed, it must have felt as though God was ignoring him. For a time, he had to sit in the frustration and discouragement of an unanswered prayer. When God finally did respond, it wasn't the answer Paul was looking for or wanted. It was an answer to a prayer God had for Paul that Paul didn't pray. But Paul could only see the full picture of what happened in this moment as he reflected back on it. While he was hearing the no from God, he must have felt confused and alone. This moment in Paul's life reaches out to any of us who have experienced that same disappointment. We find wisdom for looking at the nos we have received from God and how to view them in a new light.

When God finally responded to Paul, the words Paul heard were life-changing. Conceit was Paul's Achilles' heel, and God used this thorn to reshape his boast. Rather than continuing to parade his strengths, Paul learned to parade his weaknesses. Humility was the piece of Paul's character that God used this trial to shape. This passage can be an opportunity to reflect on what God is doing in our lives, especially with something He may be withholding. Our left-in thorns create space for us to discover the prayers God wants to answer that we haven't yet prayed.

When Paul finally looked beyond the thorn to the thorn's purpose, he realized it was there to shape his character. Even though the thorn was undoubtedly uncomfortable, it caused Paul to become more of the person God was fashioning him to be. Paul's shift in perspective caused him to stop asking for the thorn to be removed and learn to embrace what the thorn was teaching him. While I'm guessing Paul never grew to love that thorn, he accepted what God left it there to do. Our thorns take various shapes and sizes, and God allows them into our lives for what they bring out of us. Comfort is not God's ultimate goal (even though it might be ours), and sometimes discomfort is needed to bring out our best. Thorns help us see what we might not otherwise see, and be open to do what we might never choose. Looking back, we often realize our thorns are responsible for something happening in us that we would not want to have missed.

In my thorn of extended singleness and heartbreak, I held a continual prayer before God to become a mother. During the time that prayer wasn't answered, God began to teach me about the way my prayer was shaped. Like Paul, I prayed for my thorn to be removed and for my prayer to be answered the way I imagined. But during that time of singleness, God decided to answer my prayer a completely different way. Motherhood takes many shapes and forms, and God quietly spoke to my heart about all the kids around me who needed a mother. All that was required was to look at the time and desire my singleness had given me and see what God saw. I began to see those particular kids who needed someone to come alongside them and provide some extra mothering. Filling in some gaps others had left, I had the opportunity to become an answer to a bigger prayer only God saw.

When Paul described his thorn as a "messenger of Satan," he affirmed that God is not the instigator of our thorns, but allows them for what they do in us. Because Paul didn't focus his reflection on what the thorn actually was, we can substitute the thorns we've been given and glean his lessons as we contemplate our own. When thorns are not taken away, they prod us to look more closely at why God has not removed them. God edits our prayers through the Holy Spirit in ways that are designed for our growth.

With trust and acceptance, we can hold our prayers before God with an openness to the way God answers them. This frees God to sift through our prayers and occasionally reshape them into prayers He longs for us to pray. God wants us to present all our requests, and sometimes He will answer them just the way we pray them. However, when God doesn't answer them the way we want, we can look for God's answer in things that are happening in us and to us that we never would have prayed. By allowing God's no about something we want to happen, we begin to pray more for what He desires and yearns for us to see.

> Paul encourages us to see the surprising ways thorns grow our souls.

"My power is made perfect in weakness" has become a manifesto for Christ followers to find their strength in weakness. But it is the unanswered prayer regarding Paul's thorn that allowed him to come to this insight to pass on to us. The no to Paul's prayer was for a purpose that has helped believers discover the power God offers us. This bigger vision is what we make room for by offering our prayers to God and trusting God's greater plan when the answer is no. We can—and should—continue to hold our thorns before Him and ask God to remove them. But while we are called to bear them, Paul encourages us to see the surprising ways thorns grow our souls.

REFLECTION

1. Do you have any unanswered prayers or thorns in your life? In light of this passage, what could be a new prayer?

2. Can you see any reason that God may have allowed a certain thorn in your life? Has living with a thorn taught you anything that changed you or your view of God?

3. How do you balance God's value of strength in weakness in a culture that glamorizes strength, success, and perfection?

38

The Eyes of Our Heart

EPHESIANS 1:18–19

I pray that the eyes of your heart may be enlightened in order that you may know the hope to which he has called you, the riches of his glorious inheritance in his holy people, and his incomparably great power for us who believe.

"The eyes of your heart" is a phrase that is used only once in the Bible. But that image perfectly captures the vision we need for the spiritual realities God wants us to see. Our eyes on their own are incapable of looking past the things in front of us to the spiritual realities around us. Only with our heart can we grasp what God sees about who we really are. With this prayer, Paul invites us to see the riches, hope, and power God has bestowed upon us. By looking through the lens of our heart, we get a glimpse of the spiritual blessings all around us that everyone on earth will one day clearly see.

When I was a senior in high school, I had my first experience with this "inward vision." I was at a Young Life camp (for the very spiritual reason that my boyfriend wanted to go), and I heard a message that changed my life. For a moment my eyes were lifted above my high-school friends to see a glimpse of eternity, and I saw that God opened a door through Christ to anyone who reached out to Him. Though I had sat in church my whole life, I had never clearly heard this message of God's gift of grace. When I stood up to receive that grace, I had an overwhelming sense of a much bigger reality. And even though I returned to life as usual, that opening of my heart eventually led to great change. The prayer Paul offers to us here positions us before a spiritual lens that reveals that same greater reality. We get a glimpse of the spiritual blessings that are often blocked by what our distractions limit us from seeing.

> Our eyes on their own are incapable of looking past the things in front of us to the spiritual realities around us.

The Greek wording that is translated as "eyes of your heart" has to do with your mind, awareness, and inner understanding. The phrase is not meant to be taken literally, but as an image of the vision God wants us to have. Instead of seeing the world merely from the surface, Paul invites us to look deeper into the spiritual truths that have been revealed to us. With an understanding of the presence of God around us, we can see what our eyes would normally miss. We also view our circumstances and relationships differently knowing they are part of a greater reality that will last through eternity. And the way we respond to these circumstances and relationships changes with the spiritual view of them we now have.

Paul moves on in these verses to say that the eyes of our heart reveal our hope, our glorious inheritance, and God's incomparably great power. Paul builds to a crescendo with these promises, adding more Greek words as he describes all that God wants us to see. Scholars note that this oratorical style was commonly used to build intensity and fervor in order to emphasize the speaker's (or author's) point. Paul is caught up in the wonder of our spiritual blessings, and he wants to bring us into the awe he feels. If we can see what he sees, he knows we will be changed.

The hope Paul talks about is not the same word we use when we say, "I hope this happens." Our spiritual hope is not a "might" kind of hope; it is a sure hope in what God has for us ahead. Paul says God has called us into a heavenly hope not for what *may* happen, but for something that *will* happen. It is only called hope because we haven't yet seen it come to pass.

Paul speaks of the "glorious inheritance in [God's] holy people," which could be referring to the inheritance we receive from God or the inheritance God receives in us. When this term is used in other places in Scripture, it usually refers to the inheritance we are to God when we become His. But whatever way Paul means it here, he emphasizes the spiritual riches that are included in this inheritance. Different from the material wealth one would normally be left with, this inheritance will go with us when we die.

Paul moves on with momentum to the "incomparably great power" we've been given that will ultimately raise us. Death no longer holds us captive, because of the power made evident in Jesus's resurrection at work in us. This is the last and greatest spiritual blessing Paul describes, for it is the one that will propel us into eternity. It is this power that elevated Jesus to His supreme place over all rule, authority, and dominion, and it is the final crescendo of Paul's prayer.

When we see with the eyes of our heart, we become enlightened to see all our spiritual blessings. This gives us a new source of vision because we get a glimpse of what God sees when He looks at us. When our heart leads our eyes, we also have a new filter of compassion that guides our course of action. And the great power Paul describes at the end of these verses is most clearly seen this side of heaven when our eyes of love and selflessness grow to lead our lives.

REFLECTION

1. When, if ever, have you have seen through "the eyes of your heart"? What did you see?

2. Would you say that you have eyes to see the spiritual blessings God has all around you? If not, why not? If so, what are some of God's blessings that you see?

3. Which element of the spiritual blessings that Paul talks about draws you most right now: the hope we have, our glorious inheritance, or God's incomparably great power? Why?

39

Trusting the Greater Plan

PHILIPPIANS 1:12

I want you to know, brothers and sisters, that what has happened to me has actually served to advance the gospel.

Paul had the most powerful testimony of all the early Christ followers. The man who had formerly sought their death had turned and become a Christ follower himself. I imagine crowds gathered when they heard that Paul was sharing his experience. Many lives had already been changed by the words he spoke. But the powerful ministry Paul had was now constrained by a prison sentence. The lives he could continue to touch were limited to those within the reach of his chain. Nevertheless, Paul somehow had the perspective in this verse to see his imprisonment as advancing the gospel. And he proclaimed these words before having any idea how true they would be.

When our circumstances are limited and discouraging, our natural impulse is to fight against them. Paul suggests, however, that if we trust God's sovereign plan, there is another response. Paul looks beyond the frustration of his limitations to what could be happening because of his imprisonment. And with that perspective he is able to see beyond his immediate circumstances to what God might be doing with him while he is there. This perspective shift can be life-changing to our faith, because instead of just praying to get out of certain situations, we become focused on what God is doing in them. We can pray for our circumstances to change, but Paul encourages us to spend our energy and time on what God may want us to *do* while we are here. This perspective allowed Paul not only to witness to the prisoners and guards assigned to him, but to write letters to encourage the churches he could no longer visit. Had Paul not gone to prison, the New Testament might look different—because he would have been visiting the churches instead of being limited to writing to them.

What Paul *could* see was that because of his imprisonment, others were encouraged to speak the word of God more fearlessly (see v. 14). What Paul *couldn't* see was what God would do with his letters after he died. Paul saw that even though some people were preaching out of jealousy and rivalry, any preaching that was happening was spreading God's kingdom. Paul had the ability to see what God might be doing because of his discouraging circumstances, and this shows the maturity of his faith. If we believe God is in control, the frustration we feel in our circumstances is shifted to a hope of what God is doing with them. Like Paul, we can believe there is a greater story happening, and we may be where we are because we are playing an unknown part.

Because Paul did not see himself as the center of his story, he could look beyond his comfort and success and see his imprisonment in the context of God's bigger picture. Ironically, the biggest reach Paul would have was *because* of his imprisonment, and would continue long after Paul died. It was Paul's submission to

God's plan that allowed him not only to yield to his circumstances but to do what he could in in the midst of them. The way he spent his time in prison would turn out to be the legacy of Paul's life.

By writing to friends who were planting churches all over Turkey, Rome, and Greece, Paul assumed his letters would encourage the growth of those particular churches. But long after those churches died, Paul's letters would encourage millions of churches that Paul couldn't see. This reveals to us that the impact we are having could be different and bigger than we might imagine. Our impact involves not just the people we see, but the people we *don't* see who will be touched by the life we've lived. Certainly, Paul had no idea how many people would be changed and affected by his prison letters that ended up filling the New Testament. In the same way, we have no idea what person or circumstance we might impact that will set off a movement of God's grace. When we trust that we are where God wants us, even if it is not where we would have chosen to be, our response allows us to be used for God's glory. And we have no idea what even our small actions might accomplish that will stretch beyond what we know or ever see.

> The impact we are having could be different and bigger than we might imagine.

You are here on this earth because you are part of an eternal story God is writing. That perspective will either shape your life or be something you fight against when you brush up against circumstances you don't want. Not being the center of your story gives you freedom to look through your circumstances to what God may be doing in them. The circumstances you are facing might be positioning you to reach people you will never see. Paul's imprisonment allowed him not only to write letters but to experience a suffering and humility that became evident in his writings. Paul's words were fueled by the humility that Paul lived. God never wastes any of our circumstances, and we often discover in retrospect the way He used them. Paul saw that his difficult circumstances were not an accident, and he allowed God to use them for whatever God wanted them to produce.

Paul's experience teaches us that all our circumstances are for a reason, and we should do more than just pray our way out of them. We can see through the Bible that God's purpose in our circumstances might be much more than we can see. Paul did what he could in jail and trusted that God was using his life for a greater purpose. And we can thank God that Paul wrote letters of encouragement, challenge, and blessing to his friends because they were eventually included in the envelope of the New Testament for us.

REFLECTION

1. When you encounter difficult circumstances, is your first prayer, "Get me out of this circumstance" or "Show me what I need to learn through this circumstance"?

2. In most cases do you see yourself as the main character/center of your story or as a supporting character in God's bigger story?

3. Is any part of you afraid that if you embrace the message in this passage that God will somehow allow more difficult circumstances in your life? Why or why not?

40

Making the Invisible God Visible

> ### 1 JOHN 4:12
>
> *No one has ever seen God, but if we love one another, God lives in us and his love is made complete in us.*

A couple of years ago, our church passed out small blue lawn signs that said, "Love Everyone Always." Even though I was on staff, I remember hesitating when we took one, wondering what it would actually mean to put this sign in front of our door. Similar to the reason I avoid Christian bumper stickers, I imagined neighbors whispering of our hypocrisy if we ever came across as uncaring or distant. What I didn't think about was how that sign in front of our bushes would change me. Every time I came home, those words in bold orange print greeted me. They interrupted me when I had groceries fall from a poorly packed bag, an ornery teenager behind me, or a dinner I did not want to cook waiting inside. When I had a run-in with someone during the day, I found myself trying to avoid the sign's conviction as I rushed past it. The sign also interrupted my ploys for distraction when I got in my car and passed the five regular homeless people on my drive. Those three words had the effect of directing my life into a single mission. John's words in this verse have a similar effect in their quiet force.

Loving people is easy until you actually do it. For a time, it is wonderful and rewarding—until it becomes complicated and hard. Even the best relationships, after you are in them awhile, bring some level of difficulty. Other relationships are hard from the moment they begin. So as easy as loving people sounds, we need something greater than our fickle hearts to accomplish it. We know God gives us a well to draw from by extending His love to us to cover our faults. But it's the action of loving someone that generates the love we need from God to carry it out. We have to actually step out and love people to access the flow of God's love that our willingness sparks.

I have often prayed, "God, please help me love that person." That prayer has never been answered for me until I attempted to do what I prayed. There is a mystery to love in that doing it brings the power that subsequently accompanies it. This passage underlines this truth by indicating that it is *in the act of loving* that God's love appears. While this may sound confusing, it makes more sense when you think about your own experience. When you decide to love or serve, especially in a situation that is challenging, you will be met with a hundred reasons to stop before you begin. But showing up and taking that first step brings something mystical to the experience. God takes what little you have, and suddenly you find your heart filled with a love that is bigger than when you began. Your decision to love is strengthened by God's love within you that is much greater than you. Our small act of being willing is all that is needed to trigger the flow.

John says, "If we love one another, God lives in us and his love is made complete in us." The power to show the invisible God to the world is laid out in this verse. The way we love shows people whether the power of God within us is genuine. No amount of theology can prove the existence of God more than this simple act. We don't have the power on our own to do what "Love Everyone Always" requires. "Love Some People Most of the Time" is a sign we could more confidently place in front of our doors. But when we love people who are different or difficult, who support a different political party or hold a different belief, or worst of all, who have hurt us, it leads our weak heart to accomplish the miraculous. This is why John says it has the power to let God shine to the world.

This love comes with a painful price—calling us to lay down our lives and lead with humility. When we take the initiative with someone who has wronged us, it presses in hard against our pride. Loving people with opposite convictions (or social media posts that make us cringe) feels like a compromise. But in the surrounding context of this verse, we find God's love holds no conditions, and is best expressed when we go first. Verse 10 defines love by God's initiative of sending His Son to die for us. John reminds us that God did that *before* any loving behavior on our part that merited this act. Then he goes on to say that "since God so loved us" (v. 11), our response is to carry that same love to others. Taking initiative when it is *not* deserved appears to be the exact way to reflect God's love for us.

Loving people is easy when relationships are good and people do what you want them to do (which is never). Loving people is complicated when it's a sibling with a drinking problem, a blended family filled with people on opposite sides of every issue, or a coworker who drives you nuts. Loving people is a theory everyone believes in, but most of us fall short in actually doing it. Especially when the person in front of us calls out every frustration and irritation we hold in the dark part of our heart. But if we can look beyond people's issues and behaviors, we recognize

> The very person who deserves your love least presents you with your greatest opportunity.

a person usually is not acting a particular way for no reason. When we take a moment to see the pain or circumstances that might be behind the behavior, we can sometimes find the impetus to reach out with God's heart. But even if we can't find anything to move us forward, we know God reached out to us when we did nothing to deserve it. This love we hold from Him gives us the ability to love when we want to run. The very person who deserves your love least presents you with your greatest opportunity. You can make the invisible God visible when you let "Love Everyone Always" become the mission of your life.

REFLECTION

1. Think of a difficult person in your life. What is one step you could take toward loving that person?

2. Does the fact that God loves you change the way you treat people? Why or why not? When was the last time you stepped out of your comfort zone to show God's love to someone?

3. Have you ever had the experience of someone loving you when you were difficult to love? Who was it—and how did that person show you love?

Acknowledgments

For this book I'd like to thank

- Melissa Johnston, for cheering me on and helping me with the questions so I could pack this book with as much wisdom as I could
- Stacy Sharpe, who always told me I should write a book like this. Now you can pass it on!
- Kim Bangs, who patiently guided me through the initial stages and believed in this project from the start
- Earl Palmer, who was the first to open my eyes wide to God's Word
- Vivian McIlraith and Linda Strahan, who always lovingly pray me through my manuscripts
- my mom and dad, who have shown me in these twilight years that life is short
- the staff and community of Oceanhills and Peninsula Covenant Church, whom I have the joy to serve
- Brooklyn Lindsey, for the adventure of SheGrows, and for joining me in the mission of calling women to take their place in the chain of faith

And finally, a special shout-out to the two loves of my life who always sacrifice the most when I write. Jere and Jordan, I'll always be yours.

173

Laurie Short is a speaker, an author, and part of the teaching team at Oceanhills Covenant Church and Peninsula Covenant Church, both in California. She has spoken to thousands of people at conferences, colleges, and churches around the country, and her most recent adventure is becoming the visionary and co-founder of SheGrows—a cross-generational women's conference to equip and promote mentoring relationships.

Laurie is a graduate of Fuller Theological Seminary and the author of *When Changing Nothing Changes Everything* and *Finding Faith in the Dark*, as well as fourteen books for youth and youth workers.

Laurie has been in ministry for thirty years and has served on staff at four churches. She lives in Santa Barbara with her husband, Jere, and stepson, Jordan. Follow Laurie on Instagram, Facebook, and Twitter @lauriepshort.